P9-APN-081

THE FACTS ABOUT BENIGN ENLARGEMENT AND PROSTATE CANCER

Did you know:

• Prostate cancer is the second leading cancer killer of men, exceeded only by lung cancer, and the most common cancer among men, excluding skin cancer.

• More than 50 percent of men fifty and over have enlarged prostates; it is considered a normal part of aging. By age eighty, 80 percent have enlarged prostates—but only 50 percent of all men develop symptoms.

• The five-year survival rate for prostate cancer patients whose tumors are detected while still localized is 88 percent.

• One in eleven white men and one in nine black men over fifty will develop prostate cancer. At age one hundred, 100 percent of men autopsied have prostate cancer. The majority of men with prostate cancer die *with it*, not *of it.*

Here is hope and help for men with prostate problems: the latest medical, surgical, and alternative treatments, plus reassuring facts and psychological support to help men reach for recovery.

THE WELL-INFORMED PATIENT'S GUIDE TO PROSTATE PROBLEMS

THE DELL SURGICAL LIBRARY

DELL SURGICAL LIBRARY

THE WELL-INFORMED PATIENT'S GUIDE TO

PROSTATE PROBLEMS

CHARLES E. SHAPIRO, M.D., F.A.C.S., AND KATHLEEN DOHENY

A DELL BOOK

Published by
Dell Publishing
a division of
Bantam Doubleday Dell Publishing Group, Inc.
1540 Broadway
New York, New York 10036

This book is not intended as a substitute for medical advice of physicians and should only be used in conjunction with the advice of your personal doctor. The reader should regularly consult a physician in matters relating to his health and particulary in respect to any symptoms that may require diagnosis or treatment.

ISBN: 0-440-21258-8

Printed in the United States of America

Published simultaneously in Canada

June 1993

10 9 8 7 6 5 4 3 2 1

OPM

Contents

Introduction

Live long enough, so the saying goes, and a man is bound to have prostate trouble. But prostate problems are not just an old man's concern, as some people assume. With each birthday after the fortieth, the need to pay attention to this important gland becomes more vital.

For some men, the problem is prostate-gland enlargement, believed to be a natural consequence of the aging process. In other men, the problem is even more serious —cancer, either localized in the gland or also found in surrounding tissues, the bones, or in other sites.

Most disturbing to health-care professionals—and to men and their loved ones—is the rising incidence of prostate cancer. About one in eleven men will develop prostate cancer, with some ethnic groups—particularly blacks —at even higher risk, researchers say. In 1992, 132,000 men were diagnosed with prostate cancer, according to American Cancer Society estimates, and 34,000 died of it. The toll is inching up, year by year. Part of the recorded increase, some experts say, is due to better diagnostic methods, an emphasis on early detection, and the simple fact that men are living longer today. With age comes increased risk.

Consider some other disturbing statistics. Prostate cancer is now the second leading cancer killer of men, according to the American Cancer Society, exceeded only by lung cancer. It is the most common cancer among men, excluding skin cancer.

Awareness of prostate cancer has increased with news reports of public figures with the disease. In recent years, the list has grown to include U.S. Senator Alan Cranston, the rock musician Frank Zappa, and Time-Warner's late chief executive officer, Steven J. Ross, to name just a few.

Recently, U.S. Senator Robert Dole has joined the campaign to increase awareness of the risk of prostate cancer. Instead of keeping quiet when he heard his cancer diagnosis, the Kansas senator went public—and he is now pressing for an increased effort for early detection of prostate cancer. He has appeared on national television programs to discuss the disease, and he is trying to persuade his colleagues that Medicare ought to compensate older men who take screening tests to detect prostate cancer.

Some health-care experts compare men's new awareness of prostate cancer—and just how lethal it can be—to women's awareness of breast cancer in years past. Slowly, men are becoming more alert to the importance of diagnostic exams for early detection. In the same way that women know they should schedule mammograms to detect breast cancer, many men past age forty know they need an annual digital rectal exam—plus supplementary tests, in some cases—to detect prostate problems early. But because not all men are sufficiently aware, prevention-minded doctors and hospitals across the country are hosting "Prostate Awareness" weeks and offering free or low-cost exams.

Another promising development is the number of treatment and nontreatment options—ranging from "wait-and-see" to medication, radiation, and surgery. Many other treatment options are being investigated, and there is a growing awareness that psychological preparation for surgery and peer support might affect the outcome favorably.

The purpose of this book is to provide an easy-to-read, up-to-date guide to the latest information about the detection and treatment of prostate enlargement and prostate cancer. Conventional and investigational remedies are included and identified as well.

As you read through the following chapters, bear in mind that additional treatment options might now be available that were not yet ready or even under study when this book went to press. Just as important, remember that no two cases of prostate problems are the same and the best treatment for you is the one agreed upon by you and your doctor. Real-life case histories, on a first-name-only basis, are included to illustrate how others have handled prostate disorders.

HOW TO USE THIS BOOK

The best way to use this book is to view it as a source of educational and background information. It is meant to help patients with benign enlargement as well as those with cancer.

Chapter 1 includes information about prostate anatomy and a description of the prostate gland. It also includes more detailed information about enlargement of the gland, called benign prostatic hypertrophy or BPH, and prostate cancer.

Benign prostatic hypertrophy is discussed in Chapters 2 and 3. Chapters 4 through 9 are devoted to prostate cancer. The Glossary provides a quick reference to medical and other technical terms. General information about the prostate, where to write for educational materials, and other details are in the Appendix. After reading this book, you should be ready to have an informed discussion with your doctor on the range of treatment options for your particular condition and to decide the best course for you. This book is meant to help you become a successful partner with your doctor. Although treatment choices must be guided by your personal physician, knowing your options and choosing the correct one for you can reduce anxiety. And that, in turn, can pave the way for a smoother recovery.

CHAPTER · 1

The Prostate Gland

At birth, the prostate gland usually weighs only a few grams. During puberty, as the production of male hormones increases, the prostate gland begins to grow, a process that is usually complete at about age twenty. At that time, the prostate gland weighs about 20 grams, or less than an ounce.

The prostate gland is an important, if overlooked, part of the male reproductive system. The solid, walnut-shaped organ is situated in front of the rectum and just below the bladder. The main function of the prostate is to produce the seminal fluid. The gland is divided into two main areas. The inner area, which surrounds the urethra (the tube that carries urine from the bladder to the penis), undergoes benign enlargement. The outer area is the usual site of cancer formation.

During male orgasm, the muscle contractions squeeze the seminal fluid into the urethra, where it is propelled out of the penis during ejaculation.

WHAT CAN GO WRONG?

Enlargement: At about age forty, the prostate begins to enlarge. Many men do not notice symptoms of this enlargement until age fifty or older. This condition of enlargement, considered a normal part of aging, is called *benign prostatic hypertrophy* or BPH.

More than 50 percent of men age sixty and above have enlarged prostates, according to the American Foundation for Urologic Disease. By age eighty, the number with enlarged prostates reaches 80 percent. But only about 50 percent of all men develop symptoms—such as slow stream and frequent urination—due to the enlargement, and only about 10 to 20 percent of those men need an operation. When the enlargement begins to produce bothersome symptoms, there is a range of treatment options, including surgery and medication.

Prostate cancer is common in elderly men but rarely seen before age fifty. Some cases have been reported, however, in men as young as forty-five. Researchers studying prostate cancer cannot say for sure how risk can be reduced. They do know that one in eleven white men and one in nine black men over age fifty will eventually develop prostate cancer, but no one can say why black men are statistically at higher risk. Some researchers say men who have benign prostatic hypertrophy (enlargement) are more likely to develop prostate cancer, but others disagree and say that benign enlargement does not lead directly to prostate cancer.

Some researchers theorize that exposure to air pollution or to certain chemicals used in printing, painting, and shipbuilding can increase prostate cancer risk. Other research suggests that a high-fat diet might increase the likelihood of prostate cancer.

While there are no clear-cut cause-and-effect relationships, the best course of preventive action for men, researchers concur, is to undergo an annual digital rectal exam beginning at age forty. Supplementary tests, including a special blood test, may also help detect cancer of the prostate early in its course.

Despite the uncertainty about how to reduce risk, specialists agree that prostate cancer can be cured if caught in the early stages. Treatments are highly individualized, ranging from medication to radiation or surgery. A host of alternative treatments is also available and several options are in the research stages.

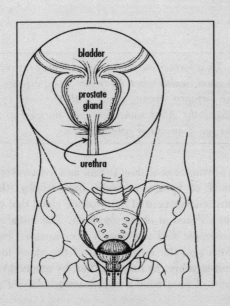

Normal Anatomy—Frontal View

CHAPTER·2

Benign Prostatic Hypertrophy (BPH):

Symptoms, Diagnosis, and Treatment

John, 75, a former engineer, was enjoying his retirement years in good health when he began to experience a slowing of his urinary stream, along with the need to urinate more frequently. After some delay, he decided to visit his doctor to see if anything could be done.

John's symptoms of slow stream and frequent urination are typical of *benign prostatic hypertrophy*, the non-cancerous enlargement of the prostate gland that typically begins in all men at about age forty. The initial changes are microscopic and not usually accompanied by symptoms. With age, the enlargement of the gland increases, slowly but steadily. As noted earlier, by age eighty, about 80 percent of men have a significantly enlarged prostate gland.

The urethra (the tube through which urine passes from

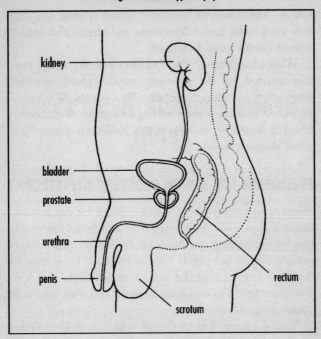

kidney

bladder

prostate

urethra

penis

rectum

scrotum

the bladder) runs through the center of the prostate gland. As the prostate enlarges, it compresses the urethra, making urination difficult, frequent, or both. In general, the more enlarged the gland becomes, the greater the obstruction of the urethra. However, some men with a markedly enlarged prostate gland have little obstruction to the flow of urine, while other men with less enlargement have a great deal of obstruction.

Typically, as the gland becomes larger, problems with urination increase. Often, there is a slowing of the urine stream. There may be hesitancy before voiding and some men notice the urine flow stops and starts. The urge to urinate comes more frequently.

What's happening? The bladder, reacting to the pressure exerted by the growing prostate gland, contracts more often and more forcefully. These contractions result in a need to urinate more often, sometimes even necessitating a visit—or visits—to the bathroom during your usual sleeping hours.

EVALUATION FOR BENIGN PROSTATIC HYPERTROPHY

When symptoms get bothersome enough for you to seek a doctor's care, your doctor probably will begin the evaluation by asking such questions as: How many times do you urinate during the night? During the day? How steady is the flow? Does it start and stop? Is it as forceful as it was a few years ago? Do you have to stand and wait before the stream begins?

Your doctor will then decide which tests are needed. These might include:

- **Digital rectal exam:** This exam helps your doctor check for enlargement of the prostate. Because the prostate lies directly in front of the rectum, it can be felt when a doctor inserts a gloved finger into the rectum. Your doctor will also check for signs of tenderness and any abnormality that may suggest a more serious problem. If necessary, other tests may be ordered. (For more information on cancer tests, see Chapter 4.)

- **Urine flow rate:** You will be asked to drink a large quantity of fluid before this test to allow your bladder to fill sufficiently. Then you will urinate into a funnel attached to a special flow meter. Using the meter, your doctor records the speed with which the stream comes out, the amount of urine passed, and the time required. The test can help determine if there is an obstruction in the urethra.

• **Postvoid residual:** Your doctor may also measure the postvoid residual, or the amount of urine left in the bladder after urinating. This measurement can be made by inserting a tube (catheter) into the bladder or by using ultrasound (an imaging technique that uses high-frequency sound waves). As a general rule, the amount of urine left should be less than three ounces (90 cc).

• **Cystoscopy:** This examination of the urinary tract is done with a special viewing tube. This test helps a doctor pinpoint an obstruction and evaluate the interior of the bladder for any changes caused by the obstruction.

• **Intravenous pyelography (IVP) or ultrasound:** These procedures are not necessary in most cases, but may be used to evaluate the kidneys to be sure there is no blockage or other problems. An IVP is a procedure for obtaining X-ray pictures of the urinary system. It involves injection of a dye into a vein in the arm. The dye travels to the kidneys and urinary tract, making them clearly visible on X rays, allowing the doctor to detect any abnormalities. Before an IVP, you will be asked not to drink fluids or eat a large meal. A laxative may also be given.

Ultrasound involves the use of high-frequency sound waves that are passed into the body to image various organs. The waves bounce off the organs and the echoes are detected and analyzed, allowing a "picture" to be composed. These tests, and possibly others, will help rule out other urinary problems such as prostatitis, urinary tract infection, or tumors of the kidneys or bladder.

TREATMENT—AND NONTREATMENT—OPTIONS

A diagnosis of benign prostatic hypertrophy does not necessarily mean that immediate treatment is necessary. Sometimes a wait-and-see attitude is the best approach. About 80 percent of men with mild symptoms decide to postpone treatment. Doctors call it "watchful waiting," because they continue to monitor symptoms without recommending a specific treatment until it is necessary.

It is important to realize that the enlargement does not invariably and progressively become worse. Be wary of a doctor who recommends an operation to relieve enlargement in the absence of objective evidence of obstruction. In fact, men often find that their symptoms will spontaneously improve. So time is not usually of the essence, unless there are changes in the urinary tract due to obstruction from the enlarged prostate. These changes can include:

- Inability to empty the bladder sufficiently.

- Visible changes in the bladder wall (called *trabeculation*) seen at the time of cystoscopy.

- Bladder-stone formation.

- Dilation of the kidneys.

In extreme cases the bladder can become completely blocked (a condition called acute urinary retention), in which case it might be necessary to insert a catheter to drain the urine. But even in this situation, an operation does not have to be done on an emergency basis, and some men can resume urinating on their own after catheter removal.

In most cases the decision to undergo an operation or other treatment depends on how much you are bothered by your symptoms. Some men who get up several times a night to urinate are not bothered enough to consider an operation, while others may wish to undergo an operation or take medicine to enjoy uninterrupted sleep.

When—and if—you and your doctor agree that treatment is needed, there are many options, both surgical and nonsurgical. You should discuss with your doctor what your options are and decide together the best course of treatment for you.

MEDICAL TREATMENTS FOR BENIGN PROSTATIC HYPERTROPHY

For some patients, medical treatment will keep symptoms of benign prostatic hypertrophy under control, at least for a time. A variety of medicines can help. They work in one of two ways: Some increase the flow of urine by relaxing the muscle tissue around the prostate and at the opening of the bladder, thus alleviating part of the blockage; others work by shrinking the prostate.

Medicines That Increase Urine Flow

These medications are approved by the Food and Drug Administration (FDA) for treatment of high blood pressure. They are not specifically approved for prostate problems, but their use for this purpose is accepted. *Terazosin* (Hytrin) is one such medicine. In early 1992, the manufacturer, Abbott Laboratories, asked the Food and Drug Administration for approval to market Hytrin as a treatment for symptoms associated with benign prostatic hypertrophy.

At the 1991 meeting of the American Urological Association, Dr. Herbert Lepor of the Medical College of Wisconsin reported on a study of Hytrin in 313 men, ages fifty to seventy-five, diagnosed with benign prostatic hypertrophy. The men took either two, five, or ten milligrams of the drug a day or were assigned to the placebo group. The drug partially relieved blocked urine flow for 59 percent of the men on the ten-milligram dose over twelve weeks. In all, 70 percent of the men on Hytrin reported a 30 percent improvement in symptoms of benign prostatic hypertrophy. But 38 percent of the men who took placebo also saw improvement. The side effects, tiredness and dizziness, were not significant, Lepor reported.

The drug can produce a rapid, marked reduction in blood pressure and care must be taken in prescribing it for prostatic enlargement, because of these side effects. To minimize dizziness, it is usually taken at night and is initiated at low doses under careful physician observation.

Another high-blood-pressure medicine used to treat the symptoms of enlargement is *prazosin* (Minipress). This is also a vasodilator drug, meaning that it lowers blood pressure by dilating, or widening, the blood vessels. It relaxes the muscles at the bladder opening, thus relieving obstruction.

Another drug in this class (called alpha-blockers) is *doxazosin* (Cardura). Among the possible side effects of all these alpha-blockers is impotence. Also, not everyone will be able to take these medications successfully. Your doctor can help assess your individual situation.

Medicines That Shrink the Gland

Drugs that relieve benign prostatic hypertrophy by shrinking the gland are used much less commonly than the blood-pressure medicines. One such class of drugs, called the *GNRH analogs,* works by preventing the biosynthesis of testosterone, the hormone that stimulates the growth of prostate cells. Most commonly, these drugs are used to treat prostate cancer. Some examples are *nafarelin acetate* (Synarel) and *leuprolide* (Lupron). These drugs are injected intramuscularly, usually monthly. The chief disadvantage is that men become impotent because of the interference with testosterone. There can be other undesirable side effects as well, including hot flashes and headaches.

Another type of medicine that works to shrink the prostate gland is *flutamide* (Eulexin). But some men who take this drug develop gynecomastia, an overdevelopment of the breast tissue. Another possible side effect is gastrointestinal upset.

Newly Available Medicines

There are also experimental and newly released drugs that shrink the enlarged gland. One of the most promising is *finasteride* (Proscar). If the drug works as well as some researchers say, many men with enlarged prostates may be able to avoid surgery, at least temporarily, by taking their daily dose of finasteride. Finasteride came on the market in 1992.

Finasteride works by blocking 5-alpha reductase, the

enzyme (a protein that regulates chemical interactions within the body) that normally interacts with the male hormone testosterone to produce dihydrotestosterone (DHT). It is dihydrotestosterone that actually stimulates the unwanted growth of the prostate.

The drug finasteride has an interesting history. Nearly twenty years ago, a medical researcher told colleagues at a conference on birth defects about a group of people living in the Dominican Republic who never developed benign prostatic hypertrophy. The researchers discovered that a genetic trait had caused a deficiency in the enzyme called 5-alpha reductase that normally interacts with testosterone to produce dihydrotestosterone. The researchers observed that the men's prostates, even after puberty, remained small. Interestingly, these men also do not develop male pattern baldness. When scientists at Merck learned of the enzyme deficiency they started their own research-and-development project.

The recent FDA recommendation that the drug is safe and effective was based on a dozen years of testing in animals and humans. In one study conducted by the Finasteride Study Group and supported by Merck and Company, the manufacturer, a dose of ten milligrams of finasteride was taken by sixty-seven men ranging in age from forty to eighty, for twelve months. A report of the study was published in the *Journal of Andrology*.

The drug does not work right away, although it does produce a rapid fall in dihydrotestosterone levels. In this investigation prostate size shrank after about six months of daily treatment. Researchers say this slow reduction is not surprising, since it takes a number of years for the gland to enlarge enough to block the urine flow.

About 70 percent of the patients in the Merck-sponsored study achieved a modest improvement in their maximum urine flow after the twelve months. The researchers concede that the increase is, at best, modest and inferior to what is achieved after surgery. Merck acknowledges that more study is needed. It is also important to note that the greatest improvement occurs in patients who had the most pronounced urinary symptoms before taking the medicine.

Overall, in clinical trials, about a third of the men taking the drug achieved "good" improvement in urine flow, according to Merck. But some urologists sound a note of caution, saying it is too soon to say if finasteride will prove to be an effective long-term treatment. One other potential problem is that the drug can lower levels of prostate-specific antigen (a protein secreted by the prostate) and make early cancer detection more difficult.

Overall, in clinical trials, about 4 percent of men taking the drug reported impotence, according to Merck, while about 1 percent of men taking placebo pills complained of it. But the impotence is reversible once the drug is discontinued and it might be coincidental.

It appears that to be effective, finasteride would have to be taken daily for an indefinite period of time. In one study, during the four-month period after stopping the drug, the prostate rapidly returned to its pretreatment size and the symptoms returned. In theory, the best time to start finasteride is before benign prostatic hypertrophy begins to develop around age forty. But not every urologist agrees this approach makes sense. The role of finasteride will become apparent over the next decade as the results of long-term use by large numbers of patients become available.

Other Approaches

Combining finasteride with alpha-blockers (the high-blood-pressure medicine already used to treat some men with enlarged prostates) may work even better, some researchers speculate. They plan to compare two approaches: alpha-blockers in combination with finasteride and finasteride alone.

SURGICAL TREATMENTS FOR BENIGN PROSTATIC HYPERTROPHY

Sometimes medical treatment does not give long-term relief. In those instances, an operation might be the best course.

For John, that was the case. At first, his doctor recommended medication to relieve the obstruction, but he got little relief. Therefore, when his doctor suggested an operation, he felt comfortable that it was the right decision.

The surgical options for treatment of benign prostatic hypertrophy follow. (For more information on anesthesia, see the Appendix.)

Transurethral Resection of the Prostate (TURP)

Transurethral resection of the prostate (TURP) is considered the "gold standard." The operation consists of inserting an instrument through the penis. The innermost core of the gland adenoma is removed, relieving the compression on the urethra. This can be likened to removing the meat of an orange while leaving the skin intact. The operation takes about a half hour to two hours with no incision in the skin.

Recently, some researchers followed up a group of men who had undergone transurethral resection and found that the procedure seemed to be associated with a higher risk of death from cardiovascular disease months later. But other experts say this finding, highly controversial in the medical community, is probably a statistical artifact.

A more recent study in the *Journal of the American Medical Association,* reported by Dr. John Concato of New York University and his colleagues from Yale University, contradicts the former study. It found that transurethral resection does not increase short-term risk of

Turp

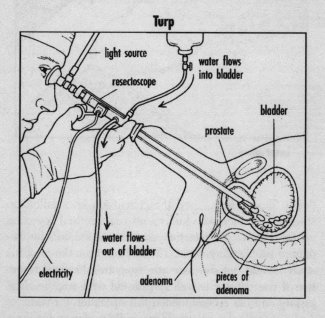

light source

water flows into bladder

resectoscope

bladder

prostate

water flows out of bladder

electricity

adenoma

pieces of adenoma

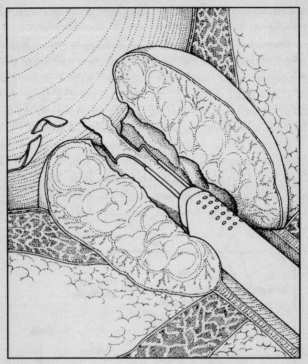

Laser view

death. Researchers based the conclusion on a follow-up study of 252 men who underwent transurethral resection versus "open" prostatectomy, another operation for benign prostate enlargement. The findings from the previous study should not dissuade you from transurethral resection if your doctor is well acquainted with your medical history and has recommended this operation for you.

Transurethral resection is generally performed using a

spinal anesthesia. Sometimes a doctor will use a general (whole-body) anesthesia, in which the anesthetics are given by injection, inhalation, or both to induce a loss of sensation and consciousness. Less often a doctor will give a local anesthesia, in which a loss of sensation is induced in and around the prostate to block pain sensations. The hospital stay for transurethral resection is usually two to four days, depending on many factors such as your general health.

Since only a part of the prostate is removed during transurethral resection, cancer might form later on in the remaining portion of the gland. Since having prostate surgery for benign prostatic hypertrophy does not make you more or less likely to have prostate cancer, as some men believe, all men should have annual prostate examinations, even if they have had prostate operations.

Transurethral Incision of the Prostate (TUIP)

Transurethral incision of the prostate (TUIP) is another surgical option. The same instrument as used in transurethral resection is passed through the penis to make a cut in the prostate to relieve the obstruction. This operation requires about a half hour to perform.

One disadvantage of this operation, however, is that since no tissue is removed, no sample can be sent to the pathology lab to do a routine check for malignancy, as it is after the resection procedure and many other operations. Also, it may be necessary to perform a TURP on patients in later years.

For that reason and others, transurethral incision isn't ideal for everyone. It works best for patients with small prostate glands. It is most often used for younger men with a relatively small amount of enlargement. Anesthesia is usually administered as a spinal or a general, or it can be local. The hospital stay may be overnight or two to four days.

Balloon Dilation

Transurethral dilation of the prostate is another option. Also called balloon dilation of the prostate, this technique works on the same principle as balloon angioplasty, which treats clogged blood vessels. The doctor first measures the length of the prostate in order to select the proper balloon size. Then a catheter with the deflated balloon tip is inserted into the urethra and positioned within the prostate. The balloon is then inflated. As it inflates, it enlarges the passage for urine flow by spreading the prostate and splitting the surrounding tissue. When the amount of dilation is sufficient, the balloon is deflated and the catheter removed. The operation takes about a half hour. The procedure can be done under spinal, general, or local anesthesia with intravenous sedation.

This technique generally provides only temporary relief. Follow-up studies of these patients suggest that about 30 to 40 percent need to be retreated. Another disadvantage is that since no tissue is removed, no sample is sent to the pathology lab to do a routine check for malignancy, as it is, for instance, with transurethral resection.

But balloon dilation can be an option for high-risk patients—such as those with serious medical problems—who might not be candidates for other operations. The procedure is sometimes done on an outpatient basis. If your doctor decides to hospitalize you for the procedure, your stay will probably be about two days.

Balloon Dilation of the Prostate

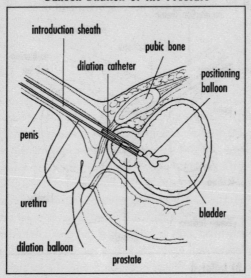

introduction sheath

pubic bone

dilation catheter

positioning balloon

penis

urethra

bladder

dilation balloon

prostate

a) Deflated

Open Prostatectomy

Open prostatectomy is yet another surgical option. This operation is usually reserved for men with very large prostates. The same tissue is removed as in the transurethral resection procedure, but it is removed via an incision made in the lower abdomen. General anesthesia is usually given, although sometimes spinal or epidural anesthesia is used. The operation takes about one and a half hours.

This operation is often recommended when there is also a need for another procedure such as hernia repair or a bladder operation. Then both procedures can be done at the same time. The hospital stay after open prostatectomy usually ranges from five days to a week.

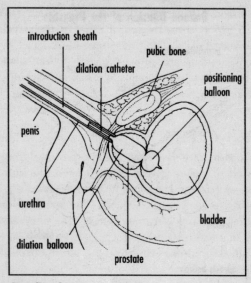

b) Inflated

Results

Since there have been no scientific studies to compare in an equal way the operations already described, there is no conclusive way to evaluate their comparative effectiveness. Such a study is under way by the American Urological Association and the federal government, but results are not expected until at least the mid-1990s. In that study, which will eventually involve twelve study sites nationwide, researchers are comparing the effectiveness of transurethral resection, balloon dilation, watchful waiting, terazosin (Hytrin), and finasteride (Proscar).

How best to treat enlargement is a matter of growing debate. The number of presentations on the topic at the American Urological Association annual meeting increased from 5 papers to 167 in just five years. Almost all patients report some degree of relief of their symptoms after any kind of prostate procedure. But the fact is, many of the symptoms are subjective and bother some men more than others, which helps to explain why comparisons of different surgical procedures are difficult.

Possible Complications of Operations

No operation is risk free, but the prostate procedures discussed so far are generally considered safe and effective. In most cases, there are no complications.

But there are risks associated with anesthetic for any operation. With general anesthesia, there is always a chance of a bad reaction to the anesthetic itself, or risk of heart attack or stroke while you are anesthetized. Spinal anesthesia also carries a risk of heart attack or stroke, but these complications are even rarer. After administration of spinal anesthesia, headache can occur. (Refer to the Appendix for more information on anesthesia.)

Other possible complications of the prostate operations discussed so far include bleeding and infection. Later, there may be scar formation (stricture) of the urethra or bladder opening. Incontinence, another possible complication, is rare, occurring in less than 5 percent of patients. When it does occur, it is generally minimal and will improve in the months following the operation. If the incontinence continues, surgical options could be considered, including implantation of an artificial urinary sphincter.

Transfusions are not usually needed, but if you have an extremely large prostate, it would be wise to discuss with your doctor before the operation the possibility of donating your own blood for storage and possible later use (called autologous blood collection). Or you might inquire about a "directed donor" collection, in which a family member or friend with a compatible blood type donates blood for your possible use later.

Sexual Effects

Men undergoing prostate procedures often wonder how—and if—their sexual function will be affected. Generally, your ability to get an erection will not change in the long run after these operations, but about 10 to 15 percent of men do have some postoperative sexual difficulties such as the inability to get or maintain an erection.

Usually the degree of difficulty in achieving an erection after a prostate operation is proportional to the presurgery sexual function. In one study published recently in the journal *Urology*, researchers from the Department of Urology at the Edith Wolfson Medical Center in Israel evaluated the effects of prostate surgery on sexual function in 210 patients. Only 12 percent of those who had normal sexual functioning before surgery reported sexual problems after the operation. The older the patient, the more likely he was to have postoperative sexual problems. Men who were in monogamous sexual relationships were also less likely to have sexual difficulties after the operation than those who did not have a regular sexual partner.

If sexual problems occur, participation in sex therapy can enhance communication between partners and the ability to obtain an erection can often be restored gradually. Other methods can also be considered. One option is oral medication that stimulates blood flow into the penis. If that does not work, vacuum-assisted erection devices can help many patients (especially those who get a partial erection) to complete and maintain an erection. More than 90 percent of patients and partners who try them are satisfied with these devices, and there are few if any complications associated with their use. The devices are usually accompanied by an educational videotape, and the manufacturers often maintain toll-free telephone numbers to answer consumer questions.

Another option is learning to inject a blood-vessel-dilating drug directly into the penis to produce an erection. If medicines and devices do not work, penile prostheses, permanently implanted, could be considered. There are several models to choose from. The simplest and most likely to work well is called a "semirigid" device. Others work on a kind of hydraulic system and are inflated when an erection is desired. But only a minority of men need to resort to the implanted prostheses to maintain an erection. Most are happy with the vacuum devices. Your urologist is well versed in all these options and will be able to give you more information.

Following the various types of operations for benign enlargement, patients do commonly experience *retrograde ejaculation*, a condition in which the sperm goes backward into the bladder instead of being propelled out from the penis. This occurs because the opening of the bladder is no longer able to constrict during ejaculation. Since the sensation of orgasm and ejaculation, however, is unchanged, this condition is not harmful or a problem unless you are trying to impregnate your partner. Retrograde ejaculation occurs routinely after transurethral resection but only in about 25 percent of patients who undergo transurethral incision.

(For information on preparation for an operation and informed consent, refer to the Appendix.)

Recovering from Operations

There is very little discomfort following TURP and
TUIP. Even so, depending on your age and other factors,
your doctor may tell you not to exercise strenuously or lift
heavy objects for three to four weeks after surgery. There
are usually no specific dietary recommendations.

Many patients will notice a pinkish tinge to the urine
immediately following the operation. That's perfectly normal. You may also experience some burning on urination
for a few days. During the course of recovery, a week or
so after surgery, blood may reappear in the urine for a
brief time. If this occurs, drink plenty of fluids and limit
your activity. Of course, if the blood seems excessive,
check in with your doctor just to be sure everything's all
right.

What about sex? Many doctors put sex in the category
of "strenuous exercise"—which elicits a laugh from some
patients—and advise abstinence for a month or so. And
remember that you still need annual prostate examinations to rule out cancer and other abnormalities.

STAYING HEALTHY

Once you recover from your operation or your medicine
begins working, you may be tempted to forget all about
your prostate gland. But to stay healthy, you need to be
alert to symptoms that might suggest the enlargement is
recurring. If you are on medical therapy, you also need to
watch for symptoms that might result from the side effects
of the drug.

You should undergo annual checkups for prostate cancer. Some men may believe that they are at less risk for
cancer of the prostate if they have undergone resection of

Finding the Right Doctor

You may initially go to your family doctor or internist for an evaluation of your prostate problems. You may then be referred to a urologist if significant benign prostatic hypertrophy is suspected.

A urologist is a medical doctor (M.D.) who is specially trained to investigate and treat disorders of the prostate, bladder, kidney, and other urinary tract organs. A urologist is adept at evaluating the severity of your condition and is attuned to the ever-changing treatment options in the field.

If you are given your choice of referrals to two or three urologists, you may wish to investigate the training of the doctors before you decide on one. If so, visit your public library and ask the reference librarian for the most recent *Directory of Medical Specialists.* Background information listed for each doctor will tell you such facts as date of birth, medical school and other training, medical school appointments, organization memberships, and board certification. If the doctor is not listed, it does not necessarily mean he or she is not qualified. Call the doctor's office and ask about the background information needed.

Another option is to call the American Foundation for Urologic Disease, (800) 242-AFUD, and ask for a listing of several urologists in your specific geographic area. You might also call your local medical society and ask for a list of qualified doctors.

Once you meet the doctor, feel free to ask questions about his or her training and general philosophy about the treatment of benign prostatic hypertrophy. If you like, obtain a second opinion from another urologist. (Your health insurance might cover this option.) It might provide you with another perspective on your condition and the best treatment for you.

the gland, but this is not true. For more information on prostate cancer tests, see Chapter 4.

RECURRENCE RATES

Keep an eye on your urinary stream. If it changes, tell your doctor. If you have undergone transurethral resection of the prostate, you might later experience blood in the urine. If so, be sure to tell your doctor.

The vast majority of people who undergo TURP need only one procedure, but the gland can grow back and cause obstruction. More commonly, regrowth causes blood to appear in the urine and in fact this blood, rather than decreased stream, is the most common reason for a second operation.

Some studies show up to 40 percent of those who undergo balloon dilation need additional treatment within a year or so. These men notice recurrence of the symptoms of slow stream that brought them to the doctor in the first place.

CHAPTER·3

Investigational Procedures for Benign Prostatic Hypertrophy

Even though a range of treatments is now available to treat benign prostatic hypertrophy, doctors are constantly searching for new therapies. These include more cost-effective surgical procedures that minimize financial demands on patients and the overburdened health-care system. In the past few years, several experimental procedures for an enlarged prostate have been considered, including a laser technique, stents (tiny tubular devices inserted permanently into the urethra), and microwave treatment.

It should be understood that these treatments, while considered promising, are still investigational. Many years of study are required before their long-term safety and effectiveness can be assured.

BPH Treatment—and Nontreatment—Options

A. "Watchful waiting."

B. Invasive (surgical) options—"tried and true"—all with low incidence of bleeding, infection, incontinence, late stricture, and other complications.

PROCEDURE	ANESTHESIA	ADVANTAGES	DISADVANTAGES	COMMENTS
Open prostatectomy	General/regional	Best relief of obstruction	Incision necessary	Reserved for large glands
TURP	same	Proven long term; tissue is obtained	Retrograde ejaculation	Is the GOLD STANDARD
TUIP	same/local	Faster, less retrograde ejaculation	For smaller glands only	Effective over long term?

C. Newer, more investigational, but still invasive option.

Laser	General/regional/local	Less bleeding	No tissue obtained, expensive	Results take 2–3 weeks

D. Newer, more investigational, less invasive options.

Balloon dilation	General/regional/local	Fast, less bleeding	Only good for small glands	Ineffective long term
Stent	Local	Fast, less bleeding	Migration? Encrustations?	Difficult removal
Microwave	None	No "surgery"	Multiple visits	How effective?

E. Pharmacologic (drug) treatments. Less effective, overall, than surgery and probably not good for long-term use.

CLASS	NAMES	ADVANTAGES	DISADVANTAGES	COMMENTS
Alpha-blockers	terazosin, prazosin, doxazosin	No surgery, treats high BP as well	Not a "cure," side effects, ongoing expense	Improvement is mostly subjective
Testosterone-lowering drugs	leuprolide, goserelin, flutamide	No surgery, shrinks prostate	Impotence	Not always effective
	finasteride (Proscar)	Prostate specific, few long-term side effects	Ongoing expense: May interfere with cancer detection	Not always effective

Source: Dr. Charles E. Shapiro

LASER-ASSISTED PROCEDURES

Two different methods of correcting benign prostatic hypertrophy involve the use of a laser to reduce tissue in the enlarged gland. The laser is an intense light beam that removes tissue without causing bleeding. This is a big advantage, since excessive bleeding is one of the main potential problems during transurethral resection of the prostate or transurethral incision of the prostate.

The type of laser beam used in the procedure is called an Nd: YAG, which stands for neodymium: yttrium, aluminum, and garnet (the components).

One laser procedure is called *transurethral ultrasound-guided laser-induced prostatectomy* (TULIP). This procedure uses a tube with an inflatable balloon at the tip, an ultrasound probe, and the laser. The tube, with the balloon deflated, is first positioned in the urethra, using ultrasound guidance. Next the balloon is inflated to compress prostate tissue, and the laser beam is directed through the balloon and the urethra (without damaging either) to strike the prostate tissue, gently burning it away. Usually, an epidural or spinal anesthesia, which numbs the lower body, is used.

A second laser procedure under study is called *laser-assisted transurethral resection of the prostate* (laser-assisted TURP). A small telescopelike device is passed through the penis. The surgeon looks directly through this telescope and inserts a laser fiber. The laser is "fired" for about sixty seconds at each of four sites. The surgery takes about fifteen minutes. A local anesthesia is usually used.

Patients selected for the laser procedures should meet the same criteria as those for standard transurethral resection of the prostate (TURP). Those criteria include a urethra that is normal, a prostate of moderate size, the absence of blood coagulation defects, and no evidence of prostate cancer.

These investigational laser-assisted procedures are often performed on an outpatient basis. The treated tissue is sloughed off in the urine over a four- to six-week period. Return to work is usually possible after one to two weeks.

These laser procedures are still investigational and additional studies are needed to determine how effective each procedure is over the long term. A disadvantage is that no tissue is obtained for examination by a pathologist.

STENTS

Also under study to treat benign prostatic hypertrophy is the use of a stent, a tubular device inserted in the urethra. Once in place, the stent pushes back the encroaching prostate, which opens the urethra and restores normal urinary function.

The stent is under study at the Mayo Clinic and other centers. Normally, patients receiving a stent can go home the same day or the next day. Most can resume normal activities almost immediately.

The concept of stents is not new. More than twenty years ago, these devices were studied as a way of preventing arteries from renarrowing after they had been opened by balloon angioplasty, a technique that allows many people to avoid coronary bypass surgery. Doctors first used these stents in peripheral arteries; next they began to insert them in coronary arteries.

One type of stent, the Prostakath, is sometimes used for short-term relief in men who cannot undergo other treatments. It is made of stainless steel coated with gold, and should not be left in place longer than six months. To insert it, a doctor uses a cystoscope, a fiber-optic device to view the bladder. Normally a patient needs only local anesthesia.

Two other types of stents, designed for permanent insertion, are now under study. One, called the UroLume Wallstent, is made of a "super" alloy material woven into mesh. It is very flexible, and self-expanding. It comes in two different lengths. A spinal or local anesthetic with intravenous sedation is administered before the stent is inserted. The other, called the Intra-Prostatic stent, is made of titanium. Since it is available in many lengths, it can be matched exactly to the length of the prostate. It is not flexible and does not self-expand. This stent is put into place after administration of a spinal anesthetic or a local

Stent

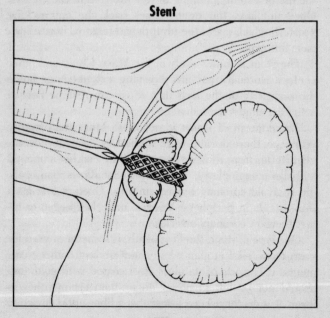

anesthetic around the prostate, combined with intravenous sedation.

In a Mayo Clinic study of the UroLume Wallstent reported in the *Journal of Andrology*, Dr. Joseph E. Oesterling placed the device in twelve patients ranging in age from sixty-two to seventy-seven years, all with obstructive benign prostatic hypertrophy. The short-term results appear promising. After three months the peak urinary flow rate nearly doubled and the postvoid residual urine volume decreased by 76 percent. There were no problems with infection, encrustation, erosion of the stent, sexual potency, or incontinence reported. Eight of the twelve patients did have frequency of urination and burning while urinating, but during the follow-up period these symptoms subsided. None of the patients needed to have the stent removed or required pain medications. Dr. Oesterling does acknowledge that additional studies are needed, using larger numbers of patients and longer follow-up.

In a study of the Intra-Prostatic stent at New York's Columbia Presbyterian Medical Center, 80 percent of men in complete urinary retention (unable to void at all) who had the stent placed were able to void spontaneously. Their peak urinary flow rate was 10.3 milliliters per second by one month after the procedure, which is considered an average level. These doctors say insertion of the titanium stent is simple and requires only several minutes. The titanium stent is considered an ideal choice for patients who cannot tolerate a more radical intervention.

In general, the major problems with stents involve the inability to remove them easily and the fact that they can migrate. The fixed size may also make it difficult to pass instruments into the bladder. In studies of the permanent stents, researchers have found that urinary flow improves without serious complications in patients. As studies continue, researchers should be able to better differentiate exactly who is—and isn't—an ideal candidate to receive the permanent stents. More study is needed, too, to determine the long-term effectiveness.

HYPERTHERMIA OR MICROWAVE TREATMENT

The use of heat (hyperthermia) to treat enlarged prostates has been suggested for about a decade and is now under study at several centers. Hyperthermia is the delivery of a controlled form of heat to a site of disease without damage to surrounding healthy tissue.

At first, efforts to use hyperthermia were directed at prostate cancer. Before long, doctors began researching the use of heat to treat benign prostatic hypertrophy in patients who were not candidates for traditional surgeries.

One device under study for heat treatment of benign prostatic hypertrophy is called a Prostatron. The power source is microwave energy. Before the heat is applied, the patient lies on a treatment table and the doctor obtains an ultrasound picture of the prostate to determine its size and shape.

Next, a catheter is inserted through the urethra to the prostate. An antenna inside the catheter transmits a dose of microwave energy that heats the prostate tissue to about 110 degrees Fahrenheit. The heat destroys some of the cells in the enlarged prostate gland. While the heat is being delivered, part of the Prostatron system flushes a coolant around the sides and end of the antenna, protecting the urethra from any heat damage.

While older microwave probes required many visits, the latest device often makes one-time treatment of about an hour possible. When the treated tissue shrinks in the weeks following treatment and the prostate gland decreases in size, more normal urinary function returns. But symptoms abate more slowly than they usually do after the transurethral resection procedure.

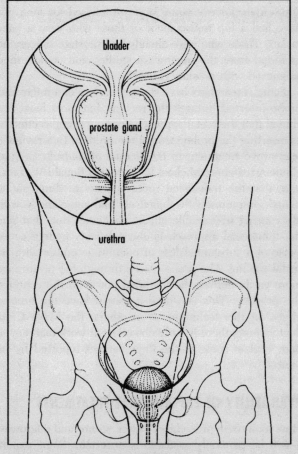

In most cases, a local anesthetic is used to deliver the microwave treatment. Patients are usually able to leave the hospital the same day. Most men are likely to feel up to resuming normal activities within just a few days. Researchers say they do not expect microwave treatment to interfere with sexual functioning, but microwave is not appropriate for everyone. It is not advised for men who have had a hip replacement or those who wear a pacemaker. Those who have already had prostate surgery are excluded from the microwave studies, too, as are those diagnosed with prostate cancer.

Some researchers have studied the use of a microwave probe inserted through the rectum, but most have concluded that the rectal approach does not seem as effective as inserting the probe through the urethra. In a review of microwave treatment in the *Journal of Andrology*, Mayo Clinic researchers Michael L. Blute and Ronald W. Lewis note that the transrectal route appears to diminish patients' symptoms both objectively and subjectively without causing irreversible effects on tissue. But, that said, the transrectal approach is also relatively inefficient because of a substantial loss of microwave power with the rectal cooling. The probe placed through the urethra can more easily deliver the intended power to the center of the prostate. This is where it should have the greatest effect. In this technique as in others, the Mayo Clinic doctors note, there is a placebo effect at work that may, in part, explain some of the improvement reported by patients.

AVAILABILITY OF EXPERIMENTAL TREATMENTS

How soon these procedures—laser, stents, and microwave —will be generally available is uncertain. Some experts predict the treatments won't be approved until the mid-1990s or later. The FDA will approve their use as "safe and effective" only after reviewing the results of extensive clinical studies.

More information about an investigational treatment can be obtained from your doctor, or call the teaching hospital in your community and ask to speak to a physician in the Urology Department. Another option is to call the National Institute of Diabetes and Digestive and Kidney Diseases, part of the National Institutes of Health, at (301) 496-3583. If the Institute knows of any clinical trials, referrals will be given.

CHAPTER·4

Prostate Cancer:
Symptoms, Screening, and Diagnosis

About 132,000 men this year will learn they have prostate cancer. Attacking one Caucasian man in eleven, according to projections by the American Cancer Society, prostate cancer is the most common cancer in men, excluding skin cancer. It is the second leading cause of death from cancer in men. For black Americans, the risk is even greater, though researchers are not sure why.

The diagnosis will be unsettling for most. But the outlook is far from bleak, especially if the cancer is detected in its early stages. One fact is well worth remembering: The majority of men with prostate cancer die with it rather than of it.

CANCER FACTS

First, some background about cancer.

"Cancer" occurs when cells grow abnormally and unrestrained in a body organ or tissue. Some cancers begin when special genes that control cell growth and division, called *oncogenes,* are transformed by *carcinogens,* cancer-causing agents. After a cell is transformed into a malignant type of cell, the change is passed on to all its offspring. This small group of abnormal cells divides more rapidly than normal cells. They are no longer capable of differentiation—that is, they do not perform the specialized tasks they are supposed to.

It can take years before the growth of these abnormal cells produces symptoms. Prostate cancer, like other forms, may actually be present for years before any symptoms become noticeable.

Age, too, plays a role in cancer development. The risk of contracting cancer continues to be low at age twenty and even age thirty. But the risk doubles between thirty and forty, some experts say, and then doubles again with each succeeding decade.

Prostate cancer is almost always a primary cancer—that is, it originates in the prostate rather than starting in another part of the body and spreading to the prostate. More than 80 percent of prostate cancers occur in men over age sixty-five. The median age at diagnosis is seventy-two years, according to the National Cancer Institute.

About 60 percent of all prostate cancers are detected while they are still localized, according to the American Cancer Society. The five-year survival rate for patients whose tumors are detected during this localized stage is 88 percent. Over the past thirty years, survival rates have improved dramatically. Since the early 1960s, the survival rates for all stages have increased from 50 to 74 percent, according to the American Cancer Society.

The longer a man lives, the greater the chance he will contract prostate cancer. At age one hundred, 100 percent of men at autopsy have prostate cancer. Between ages eighty and eighty-nine, 66 percent of men have it. Between ages seventy and seventy-nine, about 40 percent would be found at autopsy to have prostate cancer. In spite of this high incidence at autopsy, only 8 percent of men, overall, will develop a recognizable prostate cancer.

In general, prostate cancer is one of the slowest-growing cancers. Compared with breast cancer and colon cancer, for instance, prostate cancer progresses at a very slow rate. In fact, in its early development, the "doubling time" —the time needed for the tumor volume to double in size —for prostate cancer is four years. These facts are reassuring when discussing treatment options with your doctor.

Although prostate cancer most often begins to grow in the outer section of the gland, it can begin anywhere. While it might be accompanied by symptoms, usually there are no symptoms in the early stages. A man may notice a weak or interrupted urine flow, inability to urinate, or difficulty in starting or stopping the urine flow. And a man can have both prostate cancer and benign enlargement, further complicating the diagnosis.

LIFE-STYLE AND OTHER FACTORS

There are no clear-cut links to life-style patterns or medical history that can alert doctors to the presence of prostate cancer. Some research suggests that men who have benign prostatic hypertrophy (BPH) are more likely to get prostate cancer. But other researchers disagree.

For years, doctors have debated whether diet plays a role in prostate cancer (and many other cancers). Some experts believe increasing zinc intake might improve the health of the prostate. For instance, some researchers have found that prostate cancer patients have lower blood levels of this trace element than other men, but no one can say a zinc deficiency causes prostate cancer. Others say there is no concrete proof that boosting zinc intake helps.

Zinc has received increasing attention in recent years, not all of it scientifically based. Zinc is essential for normal growth, reproductive-organ development, and normal functioning of the prostate gland. It also plays a role in wound healing and the making of proteins and nucleic acids. Eating a balanced diet usually provides enough zinc. Zinc is found in lean meat and whole-grain breads, among other foods. Some strict vegetarian diets lack sufficient zinc.

Zinc supplements have been touted by self-styled nutritionists and others as remedies for everything from impotence to facial blemishes. Caution is in order. Prolonged and excessive intake of zinc, such as through supplements, may interfere with the absorption of iron and copper in the intestine. That, in turn, can lead to a deficiency of these minerals and result in headache, fatigue, abdominal pain, and anemia. Check with your doctor or a qualified nutritionist before self-prescribing zinc.

Other researchers have found that prostate cancer is directly associated with too much dietary fat. But these links were found only in one study involving only men over age seventy.

Other researchers have found an inverse relationship between the amount of vitamin A and C in the diet and prostate cancer. But vitamin A deficiency is rare in developed countries. It is found in milk and other dairy products, carrots and other vegetables, and peaches and other fruits. A balanced diet usually provides enough vitamin C as well. This vitamin is found in oranges and other fruits, green leafy vegetables, and green peppers, to name a few sources. Don't "overdo" these vitamins either. Excess vitamin C, for instance, can cause nausea, diarrhea, and other problems.

Some other studies have found that vegetarians and men who eat little meat have a lower frequency of prostate cancer. There is also debate about how obesity might influence prostate cancer, with some researchers saying excess weight might increase risk.

Family history of prostate cancer plays a role in risk, but researchers disagree about how large a role. Your doctor is likely to ask if your father, uncles, grandfather, brothers, or other family members had prostate cancer. In a study of 385 prostate cancer patients and the same number of patients without prostate cancer (who served as the control group), researchers recently found that the overall risk for men with a first-degree relative (father or brother) with prostate cancer was elevated. The study appeared recently in the *Journal of Urology.* Risk is also elevated, but not as much, for men whose grandfathers or uncles had prostate cancer.

Another investigation, led by Dr. Gary D. Steinberg of the James Buchanan Brady Urological Institute, found that men whose fathers or brothers had prostate cancer were twice as likely to develop prostate cancer as men with no relatives affected. They based the study, published in *The Prostate,* on nearly 700 men with prostate cancer and more than 600 control-group patients.

A 1990 report linking vasectomy and prostate cancer concerned many men, but the researchers say they cannot necessarily call vasectomy a risk factor for prostate cancer. In the study, reported in the *American Journal of Epidemiology,* Dr. Curtis Mettlin and his research team at Roswell Park Cancer Institute in Buffalo, New York, reviewed the records of more than 3,000 patients with prostate and other cancers. They found the rate of prostate cancer, present in 610 men, was twice as high for men who had undergone vasectomies more than a dozen years before their cancer was diagnosed. The researchers emphasize that they established an association but not necessarily a risk factor. To medical researchers, these are two different phenomena. An association is a close relationship between two events or characteristics; a risk factor is a clearly defined occurrence associated with the increased rate of a disease that subsequently occurs.

MAKING THE DIAGNOSIS

If a prostate abnormality is suspected, a physician will ask for details about your medical history and perform a series of examinations and tests. Some or all of the following tests might be ordered.

Digital Rectal Examination

The *digital rectal exam* is the best starting point in detecting both enlargement of the prostate and cancer of the gland. A doctor uses a gloved finger to examine the inside of the rectal area to try and detect a hard lump or growth in the prostate gland, which can be felt through the rectal wall. If anything suspicious is detected, additional tests will be ordered.

Prostate-Specific Antigen (PSA) Assay

The *prostate-specific antigen* (PSA) *assay* is a blood test that some—but not all—experts say is twice as accurate as a digital rectal exam in detecting cancer. Prostate-specific antigen, or PSA, is a protein produced by prostate cells.

PSA is produced by normal prostate cells as well as cancerous ones, but the amount of PSA in the blood can increase when prostate cancer is present. This test is not foolproof, however. In a man with a healthy prostate, the normal values on a PSA test vary with the type of test used.

At a recent conference on prostate cancer sponsored by the American Cancer Society, it was reported that elevated PSA levels are often the result of nonmalignant problems like benign prostatic hypertrophy, prostatitis, and recent rectal examination. It is therefore important to remember that the result of the PSA test is just one piece of information that helps detect prostate cancer.

The PSA should be done early in the investigation of suspected prostate cancer. The initial level serves as an important "baseline" value; follow-up test results can be compared to this initial test.

Prostatic Acid Phosphatase Test

The *prostatic acid phosphatase* (PAP) *test* is a blood test that detects prostatic acid phosphatase, an enzyme that can become elevated in the presence of prostate cancer. Because the PSA test is more sensitive, it has largely replaced the PAP test.

Transrectal Ultrasound

This special ultrasound technique reveals abnormalities too small to be detected by physical digital examination. First, an instrument is inserted into the rectum. Sound waves are directed toward the prostate and bounce off it. With the help of a computer, the pattern of the echoes made by the sound waves is converted into a picture. This picture helps your doctor detect areas that are abnormal.

Biopsy

To confirm the diagnosis of cancer, your doctor may recommend a *biopsy,* the surgical removal of a small tissue sample for examination under a microscope to see if cancer cells are present.

Tissue is removed with a needle placed directly into the prostate gland, usually through the rectum. This procedure is most often done with a local anesthetic.

Transrectal ultrasound may be used to guide the needle to the proper site. How uncomfortable is it? One man, who admitted he might be braver than most, said the biopsy was "no worse than getting a shot." As with any test, there is always a chance of bleeding or infection. To minimize these risks, do not take aspirin for two weeks before the biopsy. A short course of preventive antibiotics will be given before and after the biopsy.

DEBATE OVER TESTS

There is much debate over which of these tests, alone or in combination, is the most reliable in screening men for prostate cancer. Much of the debate centers on whether the PSA test should be used as a routine screening test.

In late 1992 the American Cancer Society issued new guidelines recommending annual PSA tests beginning at age fifty, or earlier for high-risk men.

Some researchers say the PSA test will help detect cancer in its earliest and curable stages and should be done routinely, even if no cancer is suspected. But others cite costs, which would be substantial on a nationwide level if every man over age forty were to take the test. It is even possible that widespread use of this test might do more harm than good by leading to the detection of microscopically small cancers that will not grow large enough to become significant during a typical lifespan. A man might therefore undergo a radical prostatectomy to remove a small cancer that would never have been life threatening.

Reports in medical journals offer conflicting conclusions. Researchers from the Hôpital de l'Antiquaille in France recently compared the rectal exam with the PSA test and transrectal ultrasound in 863 men and reported their findings in the *British Journal of Urology*. They concluded that the rectal exam "is currently as useful an examination as any in the detection of asymptomatic prostatic cancer." They added that ultrasound should not be used as a screening tool, but said it doubled the detection rate as a second test if the prostate felt abnormal during the digital rectal exam. They contend that the PSA test alone is "valueless" as a screening tool, but it can be helpful once an abnormality is detected.

Not everyone agrees with the French researchers. Another study, reported in the journal *Urology* by researchers at Tulane University and the Veterans Affairs Medical Center in New Orleans, found the PSA test highly useful in detecting prostate cancer in younger men. They evaluated 414 men between ages forty and fifty-nine by using a questionnaire, a rectal exam, and a PSA test. Ten patients in the fifty-to-fifty-nine age group had elevated PSA tests; five eventually were found to have cancer.

In the *New England Journal of Medicine* Washington University researcher William J. Catalona reported that the combination of three detection methods—PSA, follow-up biopsy, and rectal exam—provides a better detection method than rectal exam alone.

Some doctors believe the digital exam and ultrasound should both be used for routine screening and that the PSA test should be used if anything appears suspicious on the first two tests. The entire argument is complicated by the fact that prostate cancers in different individuals can grow very differently, and doctors cannot easily predict which cancer will grow more quickly.

Options in Screening for Prostate Cancer

Test	Description
Digital rectal exam	Doctor inserts gloved finger into rectum; can feel for abnormalities in prostate through rectal wall.
PSA	A blood test that detects a protein secreted by the prostate. Elevated levels might indicate cancer, but not always.
Transrectal ultrasound	Takes a "picture" by bouncing sound waves off the interior of the prostate gland and converting them into an image. Careful evaluation of the image can detect abnormalities.
Biopsy	Removal of a tissue sample that is examined for the presence of cancer cells.

ADDITIONAL TESTS

If the biopsy proves cancer is present, the next step is to determine if the disease has spread (metastasized) beyond the prostate gland. This process is called "staging" and it helps your doctor decide on the best treatment.

The first and most useful test is the determination of the PSA level. Besides serving as a "baseline" for later comparison to monitor treatment effectiveness, the PSA level can indicate the likelihood of the tumor having spread outside the prostate.

Because prostate cancer can commonly spread to the bones, a bone scan is usually ordered. In this test, a small amount of a radioactive substance is injected into a vein in the arm. This radioactive substance collects in areas of abnormal bone activity. Then a scanner pinpoints those areas, recording them on X-ray film. It is often difficult to distinguish arthritic changes from cancer and from areas of prior injury. Where ambiguities exist, X rays of suspicious areas may be required.

Your doctor may also order a CT or CAT scan, a series of X rays taken as a scanner revolves around you. The images create a cross-sectional picture of the body area being scanned and can reveal lymph-node enlargement or the spread of the tumor into adjacent tissues.

A relatively new procedure called *flow cytometry* determines the amount of DNA, or genetic material, in prostate cells removed during the biopsy. It measures the cells' fluorescence (ability to give off light) after they have been stained with dyes that attach themselves to the DNA.

With this test, doctors can identify characteristics of cancer cells that appear to be related to the growth rate of the cancer. Although now in limited use, this test is expected to be used increasingly to help doctors plan treatment.

STAGES

Depending on its extent, prostate cancer is divided into stages. Two staging systems are in common use. One classifies cancers from stages A through D, with cancer in stage A the smallest and least invasive. Another system is called the TNM system. T stands for tumor size, N for the degree of spread to the lymph nodes, and M for the presence of metastasis. A number is added to each letter to further indicate the size of the tumor and its spread.

In the stage-A-through-D system, stage A prostate cancer involves a tumor that is not detectable by any of the routine tests but has been found during an operation for presumed benign enlargement of the prostate, such as transurethral resection of the prostate (TURP). Up to 10 percent of men having a TURP will be found to have cancer in the removed tissue. Stage B means the tumor can be felt by rectal exam but has not spread beyond the prostate gland. Stage C prostate cancer has spread beyond the prostate to nearby tissues. Stage D cancer has spread to the pelvic lymph nodes or distant parts of the body. Most commonly the spread is found in the bones.

An expanded version of this staging system is sometimes used. It further divides the stages into three or more substages. The accompanying list describes the stages and substages in further detail.

Stage A: Although present in the prostate, the cancer feels like normal prostate tissue during a digital rectal examination; cancer cells are found after a transurethral resection of the prostate.

Stage A1: Cancer cells at this stage look more like normal cells than fast-growing cancer cells do. Doctors call cancer cells in this stage "well differentiated." In contrast, poorly differentiated cancer cells are more disorganized; they grow much more quickly. Also in stage A1, the amount of tumor is less than in stage A2.

Stage A2: Cancer cells are poorly differentiated or they are present in many areas of the prostate gland.

Stage B: The cancer is still localized, confined within the "capsule" of the prostate. At this stage, a doctor can feel it during a digital rectal examination.

Stage B1: The cancer is confined to one side of the prostate and is no larger than about five eighths of an inch.

Stage B2: The cancer is more extensive than in stage B1 or involves both sides.

Stage C: The cancer is in the prostate and has spread to nearby tissues or the seminal vesicles, or both. The seminal vesicles are extensions of tissue from the prostate and lie under the bladder. They produce a portion of the seminal fluid.

Stage C1: There is minimal extension of cancer to tissues surrounding the prostate.

Stage C2: There is more extensive cancer spread to nearby tissues. There is often urinary obstruction.

Stage D: The cancer is found in regional lymph nodes or is believed to have spread beyond the pelvic area to the bone or to other organs.

Stage D0: There are no clinically identifiable areas of spread (metastasis), but blood tests such as prostate-specific antigen (PSA) or prostatic acid phosphatase (PAP) are elevated.

Stage D1: The cancer is found in the regional lymph nodes.

Stage D2: The cancer is found in distant lymph nodes, the bones, or other faraway organs.

Stage D3: The cancer has progressed even after hormone therapy has been given.

Source: National Cancer Institute

The accompanying list provides an overview of the TNM system.

T0: Technically called *carcinoma in situ,* the malignant cells are found lining the inside of the gland. T1 is used to describe the smallest tumor. T2 through T4 are used for larger tumors.

N0: The nearby lymph nodes are free of cancer. N1 through N3 are used to denote the increasing degree of involvement of regional lymph nodes.

M0: No distant spread of cancer cells has been found. M1 would denote spread, or metastasis.

GRADING

Grading, based on microscopic appearance of the cells, can also help your doctor decide the best treatment for you by predicting how aggressively the tumor might spread.

Probably the best known is a system called the Gleason grade, which classifies the cancer cells on a scale of 1 to 5. The lower the Gleason grade, the more differentiated the cells. Poorly differentiated cells are believed to grow more quickly than well-differentiated cells.

If the grades are low, from 1 to 2, the cells are well differentiated. If the grade is intermediate, 3, the tumor has moderately differentiated cells. The highest grades, 4 and 5, are given to the most poorly differentiated cells.

The Gleason grade is related to the volume of the tumor and can be particularly helpful in predicting progression.

TREATMENT DECISIONS

Once all this information is gathered, your doctor is in a better position to suggest the best treatment, based on the amount of cancer found, the Gleason grade, the location, your age and general medical condition, and other factors.

Men who are over age sixty and found with stage A1 prostate cancer (typically when their doctor performs a transurethral resection [TURP] to reduce an enlarged prostate) often are advised not to have surgery but simply to return for regular checkups. This is recommended because the cancer usually grows very slowly. But younger patients with stage A1 may be candidates for radical prostatectomy surgery (in which the gland is removed) or for radiation therapy.

In general, men with stage A1 prostate cancer will have a life expectancy similar to that of the general population, according to the National Cancer Institute. Prostate cancers classified as stage B are often treated by radiation or surgery. Cancer that has spread is often treated by hormonal therapy or chemotherapy (anticancer drugs). Each of these treatments is discussed in greater detail in the following chapters.

Age is a consideration in treatment decisions, but not the only one. In a study conducted by researchers at the UCLA School of Medicine, the Rand Corporation, and the New England Medical Center and published recently in the journal *Cancer*, the researchers reviewed the charts of nearly 250 prostate cancer patients. They found that older patients, seventy-five years and above, were less likely to undergo surgery and radiation than younger patients. Treatment decisions should not be based solely on age and the extent of the cancer, they conclude, but also on life expectancy and the ability of the patient to tolerate the various procedures and treatments, and on how the procedures and treatments could affect the quality of the individual's life.

Hearing a diagnosis of cancer is never easy. Few people grasp everything a doctor says during the visit. No matter how optimistic a patient, news of cancer can be overwhelming.

John, a fifty-eight-year-old technician, decided to go to a prostate screening program at his workplace after a co-worker had told him about it. When the doctor did a digital rectal exam, he felt something "suspicious." He sent John to his regular doctor, who referred him to a urologist. The urologist conducted more tests, including a biopsy.

While he waited for all the test results, John tried to put the whole idea of cancer out of his mind. He felt confident that everything would be fine. His optimism, he said later, made hearing the diagnosis even more difficult. He could not believe his ears when the doctor confirmed that he had cancer of the prostate.

It is not easy for anyone to hear a cancer diagnosis, and it is not an easy time to absorb so much technical information. Patients should therefore feel free to telephone the doctor or to return with a list of questions. Asking family members or friends for input may bring up important questions that have not occurred to you.

Getting a second opinion might be in order. See the Appendix for more information on how to do so.

After his doctor told him he had Stage B2 prostate cancer, John went to the public library. "I read about a dozen books and several magazine articles," he said. "It was my way of educating myself and by doing so, I felt more in control of the situation."

MEN AT HIGH RISK

Men who are at high risk of developing prostate cancer might want more information about a National Cancer Institute–sponsored study now in the planning stages. In the study, expected to involve sixteen thousand men, half the subjects will be given finasteride (Proscar) to determine what effect, if any, the drug has on cancer prevention. (See Chapter 2 for more information on Proscar.) Half will serve as control patients, says Dr. Barnett Kramer of the NCI. The study leaders will especially recruit black men, known to be at higher risk for prostate cancer than other ethnic groups. (For more information on clinical trials, see the Appendix.)

CHAPTER·5

Treatment of Localized Prostate Cancer

Joe, 64, was upset when his doctor told him he had prostate cancer. But his doctor followed the bad news with some reassuring information. According to the tests and scans, his cancer was believed to be confined to the gland. He was a perfect candidate for an operation—and the doctor was fairly sure the operation would eliminate the cancer completely.

Many cases of prostate cancer are similar to Joe's. Most often the cancer begins in the so-called "peripheral" or "posterior" portion of the prostate, the section that lies just beneath the rectal wall. This explains why the digital exam is the best way to detect the tumor.

A patient with prostate cancer in an early stage and localized to the gland is a candidate for curative therapy, either an operation or radiation therapy. There are several options with each approach.

RADICAL PROSTATECTOMY

One surgical option is *radical prostatectomy,* the removal of the entire prostate gland and surrounding tissues. This treatment is most likely to be recommended for medically fit patients who have a life expectancy of ten years or more and whose cancer is confined to the gland.

There are several ways to perform the surgery. *Radical retropubic prostatectomy* is one technique. The surgeon makes an incision from below the navel to the pubic bone, or horizontally across the lower abdomen, and removes the entire prostate gland and the pelvic *lymph nodes.* (Lymph nodes are part of the body's lymphatic system, found all over the body and involved in the immune system.) Prostate cancer usually spreads first to the lymph nodes adjacent to the prostate gland, the so-called "pelvic lymph nodes."

For retropubic prostatectomy, general (whole-body) or epidural (spinal) anesthesia is most often given. (See the Appendix for more information on anesthesia.)

The surgery itself takes about three to five hours. The patient is hospitalized for about a week and usually goes home with a catheter in place. Before radical prostatectomy, your doctor might suggest that you donate three to five units of your own blood, since in most cases transfusions will be needed. This is called "autologous" blood donation.

During this operation the prostate is cut away from the bladder opening and from its attachment at the urethra. The bladder is then sewn down to the urethra and a catheter is left in place for two to three weeks while healing takes place.

Because the entire prostate gland and the tissues around it are removed, impotence has been a usual consequence of this operation. However, in 1982, doctors developed a modified approach to the radical retropubic prostatectomy. The new approach is popularly called the "potency-sparing" technique because it leaves intact the nerve bundles and blood vessels responsible for getting and maintaining an erection. But a "potency-sparing" procedure should not be a "cancer-sparing" procedure. It is feasible only in some cases, particularly if the tumor is not large and if it is confined to one side of the prostate.

Generally, younger patients are likely to be more sexually active than older patients and to have smaller tumors so they have a better chance of having their potency preserved.

In a study reported in the journal *Urology*, researchers at Ohio State University followed 151 men for one year who had had a nerve-sparing prostatectomy, and found potency had returned in 66 percent of the cases. The return was indirectly related to age and to the stage of disease, with return more likely in lower-stage disease and younger patients.

(For more information on sexual rehabilitation, see Chapter 9.)

The surgeon performing a radical retropubic prostatectomy usually samples the lymph nodes before removal of the gland. The purpose of this procedure, called a *pelvic lymphadenectomy*, is to determine if cancer has spread to the lymph nodes. If it has, the surgeon will probably not remove the gland, because once the tumor is found outside the prostate, removing the gland offers little likelihood of a cure. This possibility should be discussed with your doctor ahead of time.

A new technique of lymph-node sampling is called *laparoscopic lymphadenectomy* (LALA). In this procedure, a telescopelike device called a laparoscope is inserted through a small opening in the abdomen and is used to guide the sampling of lymph nodes. General anesthesia is required.

Radical perineal prostatectomy, another surgical approach to removing the prostate gland, is gaining in popularity with the advent of LALA. In the radical perineal prostatectomy, an incision is made between the scrotum and the anus, enabling the surgeon to remove the gland and surrounding tissues. This technique, usually done with general anesthesia, requires only about one or two hours, compared with the three to five hours usually required for the radical retropubic prostatectomy. The shorter operating time is an advantage, especially for men with chronic medical problems such as heart or lung disease. The disadvantage of LALA and radical perineal prostatectomy is that two separate operations are needed.

For a radical perineal prostatectomy, your doctor will probably arrange for your admission to the hospital the evening before the operation. Your doctor might also suggest that you donate a couple of pints of your own blood ahead of time in case a transfusion is needed. You will probably stay in the hospital three to six days and you will be sent home with a catheter in place.

Other Possible Complications

Postoperative urinary incontinence is a legitimate concern of men facing radical prostatectomy. It affects virtually everyone, especially right after the catheter is removed. But the problem is most often only temporary, with over 90 percent of men achieving acceptable continence within a year of the operation.

Before the operation, the anesthesiologist will meet with you to describe the procedure. Either an anesthesiologist or a nurse-anesthetist working under a doctor's supervision will give the anesthesia and stay with you for the entire operation. (See the Appendix for more information on anesthesia, informed consent, and preparation for an operation.)

RADIATION THERAPY

Treatment with radiation involves the application of high-energy particles to destroy cancer in the tissue. It has been used for prostate cancer since the early 1900s. Radiation can be delivered externally by a machine or internally by implanted radioactive pellets.

External beam radiation is usually given five days a week for six or seven weeks. The aim is to deliver the maximum dose to the gland while minimizing exposure to the bladder and rectum. A CT scan can often help determine the appropriate radiation field.

During treatment, you may experience inflammation of the bowel and bladder, which can cause diarrhea and frequency of urination with some burning. Your doctor can give you medicines and suggest special menus to help until these side effects subside, usually within three months. Some gastrointestinal and urinary-tract complaints may continue beyond that time, but not often. Because of possible bowel problems with radiation therapy, this approach is not recommended for anyone with inflammatory bowel disease.

About half the patients who have external beam radiation become sexually impotent, usually six months after treatment is ended. It is probably the result of direct radiation injury to the small vessels and secondary damage to the pelvic nerves.

Another approach to radiation therapy is implanted, or

"interstitial" radiation. Also known as "brachytherapy," it involves the implantation of pellets of radioactive material that deliver the radiation directly to the cancer cells. Interstitial radiation therapy was introduced more than two decades ago.

For this procedure, fifty or so tiny "seeds" of a radioactive substance, each the size of a rice grain, are implanted in the prostate, usually via an incision. The advantage of this delivery over an external one is that it is more concentrated and the lymph nodes can be removed and examined at the same time for more accurate staging of the cancer.

The implants do not have to be removed. They slowly "burn out" and become less radioactive. Recently, techniques to place removable seeds under ultrasound control (without the need for an incision) have been under study.

The pellets or seeds for implanted radiation are made of such elements as iodine (I-125), gold (Au-198), iridium (Ir-192), or palladium (Pd-103). Because gold implants have higher-energy radiation, they cause greater tissue degeneration. More recently, implants of palladium have been introduced, for which some researchers claim superior results.

Side effects vary with the kind of implant. There might be bowel and urinary-tract side effects, as with external beam radiation. Impotence can occur.

Since the seeds are implanted directly into the prostate, a surgical incision is usually required. Your urologist works closely with your radiation therapist to plan and carry out the procedure. You will be asked to sign an "informed consent" form. For more information, refer to the Appendix.

COMBINATION TREATMENT

Sometimes follow-up radiation therapy is prescribed for patients who have undergone prostatectomy, especially if it was not possible to remove the entire tumor or if the tumor recurs in the area of the prostate after the operation.

SURGICAL TREATMENT VERSUS RADIATION TREATMENT

For years, doctors have debated the benefits of surgical treatment versus radiation treatment. Because most studies show surgery results in a lower likelihood of recurrence, many experts feel radiation therapy may not treat the cancer as effectively. However, this must be weighed against the advantages of radiation. It does not require an operation and is less likely to cause incontinence.

The variety of options can make the choice of treatment difficult. Discuss the advantages and disadvantages of each approach with your urologist and radiation therapist so that your choice of treatment is based on a thorough knowledge of the facts.

WATCHFUL WAITING

Remember that prostate cancer is very common and that every man will get it if he lives long enough. Usually, but not always, the tumor tends to be slow growing. Therefore, the majority of men who develop prostate cancer will die with it, not of it. Most experts would say not to treat localized prostate cancer aggressively unless the patient is in good health and has at least a ten-year additional life expectancy. For some patients, usually older and possibly in poor health, the doctor may recommend that they be observed and hormonal treatment be prescribed when and if necessary. For more information, see Chapter 6.

SPECIAL CASES: MEN UNDER AGE FIFTY

Prostate cancer usually strikes men over age fifty. In fact, only 1 percent of those diagnosed with prostate cancer are younger than age fifty. But researchers who have taken a closer look at this group have discovered that their cancer seems to be more virulent. Some doctors have noticed an increase in younger prostate cancer patients, but this increase might be the result of greater awareness of the need for physical exams. These younger, healthier men have a long life expectancy and should be treated aggressively, usually with radical prostatectomy.

MONITORING TREATMENT AND PREDICTING RECURRENCE

In addition to helping with the initial detection of prostate cancer, the prostate-specific antigen (PSA) blood test plays an important role in monitoring disease during and after treatment. Since PSA is made only by prostate cells, it will be undetectable if all prostate tissue is removed by surgery or destroyed by radiation. If PSA reappears or begins to rise following radiation or surgery, then prostate tissue is present somewhere in the body and might signal return of the cancer.

In a report published in the *Journal of Urology,* researchers conclude that the PSA test, rather than the digital rectal exam, is an "excellent early indicator of possible local recurrence after radical prostatectomy." The team from the University of Minnesota and the Veterans Ad-

ministration Medical Center in Minneapolis base the conclusion on the evaluation of recurrent cancer in sixty-three
patients.

Patients treated with external beam radiation whose
PSA levels do not return to the normal range within a year
after the conclusion of treatment are at high risk for tumor
recurrence, according to another report in the *Journal of
Urology*, based on a study of 143 patients done at five
different medical centers.

(Treatment options for recurrent cancer or cancer that
spreads outside the prostate are discussed in the next
chapter.)

SURVIVAL RATES

If prostate cancer is detected while localized to the gland,
the outlook is very good. More than 88 percent of patients
make it to the five-year survival stage, according to the
American Cancer Society. Many men end up "outliving"
their prostate cancer, dying of old age and other causes.
About 87 percent of patients with early-stage prostate cancer who undergo radical prostatectomy are disease free at
the fifteen-year mark. The survival rates of those who undergo radiation therapy are comparable, but the surgery
patient might have higher cancer-free survival rates, some
studies show.

SECOND OPINION

Before consenting to an operation or other treatment, you
might wish to obtain a second opinion. See the Appendix
for more information.

Bill got a second opinion and then felt comfortable undergoing the radical prostatectomy recommended by the first doctor he saw. "At my age," he said, "I thought it was better to just get it over with and take it out."

He stayed in the hospital for eight days and then relaxed at home, gradually increasing his activity. He has resumed an active life-style. He tries to walk two miles two or three times a week and plays golf at least once a week.

CHAPTER·6

Treatment of Advanced Prostate Cancer

In advanced prostate cancer, the disease has spread, or *metastasized*. The concept of metastasis was first discussed extensively by a French physician in 1829. Before his writings on the subject, doctors knew that cancer cells were found outside their original site, but many believed that these other tumors were new, independent cancers. Now scientists are zeroing in on how and why a cancer spreads. In time, they hope to develop better treatments to arrest or prevent metastases.

HORMONE TREATMENT

Prostate cancer grows in response to the main circulating male hormone, testosterone. Even when prostate cancer is in advanced stages, hormone therapy is very effective. This treatment approach can also be used if the disease recurs after surgical or radiation therapy or when the tumor is localized but too large to remove.

Although many options exist, the underlying rationale in each case is the same: to deprive the tumor of testosterone, without which the prostate cancer cells cannot grow.

While hormone treatment is not a cure, it can very reliably cause the tumor to go into a remission. Although the length of a remission depends on the individual tumor, it can commonly last for years. When the tumor goes into remission, bone pain disappears, appetite returns, and weight is regained. Urinary symptoms can also improve. All treatment that lowers the male hormone, however, will cause impotence and sometimes hot flashes. Rest assured, your voice will not change. You will still need to shave. (For more information on impotency and sexual rehabilitation, see Chapter 9.)

ORCHIECTOMY

Orchiectomy is an operation to remove the testes. It is the oldest form of hormone treatment for prostate cancer, and no other form of hormonal therapy is any better. The surgery itself is low risk, but it does require removal of both testes. It is usually performed on an outpatient basis using local anesthesia.

During the surgery, the scrotum (the pouch containing the testes) is opened and the testes are removed. The skin is stitched back together. After surgery, painkillers may be prescribed and ice may be applied to the area to minimize swelling.

ESTROGEN THERAPY

Another approach is hormone medication. The female hormone *estrogen* can be given to reduce or eliminate production of testosterone. A synthetic form of estrogen called *diethylstilbestrol* (DES) can be prescribed, but this drug has largely been replaced by other forms of hormone treatment. Similar to orchiectomy, estrogen will cause impotence and loss of sex drive, but because it is a female hormone, it will also cause breast enlargement and tenderness. Some doctors order radiation to the breast before beginning estrogen treatment. The association between high estrogen doses and cardiovascular problems is another reason estrogens have been largely replaced by other forms of hormone treatment for advanced prostate cancer.

LHRH AGONISTS

Like estrogen, the drugs known as *luteinizing hormone-releasing hormone* (LHRH) agonists suppress testosterone production. Normally, LHRH is released by the brain and controls the production of male and female sex hormones. The LHRH agonists interfere with the action of LHRH, resulting in a low level of testosterone production.

Two such agonists are approved by the FDA: *leuprolide* (Lupron) and *goserelin* (Zoladex).

The "depot" form of leuprolide is given by injection that slowly releases the drug for twenty-eight days. Goserelin is given only by implanted pellet and also lasts for about one month. These agonists do not cause breast enlargement, but they do result in impotence and sometimes hot flashes. Leuprolide can also cause headaches, nausea, and vomiting. Goserelin can result in constipation or diarrhea along with nausea and vomiting.

John, 58, is receiving combination hormone therapy. The treatment is not without its inconveniences. "I do have hot flashes," he said, "sometimes every hour." Still, he manages to hold down his full-time job as a technician, working the evening shift.

A study published in the *British Journal of Urology* found no difference in the two-year survival between patients treated with goserelin and those treated by orchiectomy. The English research team followed up 358 men, randomized to receive either medical or surgical treatment. The treatments were equally effective in decreasing testosterone concentrations.

ANTIANDROGENS

Another kind of hormone treatment involves the use of *antiandrogens,* which inhibit the action of testosterone on prostate cancer cells. A relatively new antiandrogen is *flutamide* (Eulexin), approved by the FDA in 1989 for use in combination with leuprolide for advanced prostate cancer. The combined therapy might lengthen survival time and might also provide better pain relief, although in some cases the addition of flutamide has resulted in breast enlargement and gastrointestinal upset. Flutamide may also help men whose cancer recurs after orchiectomy.

CHEMOTHERAPY

For prostate cancer, *chemotherapy* is often considered a last-resort treatment. Chemotherapy is the use of chemicals or drugs specifically designed to kill or suppress the cancer cells.

Among the chemotherapy agents used to treat prostate cancer are *5-fluorouracil and doxorubicin.* Using two drugs together, some researchers say, may work better than single-drug treatment. Recently, researchers from several institutions reported success in combining *estramustine phosphate sodium* (Emcyt) and *vinblastine sulfate* (Velban, Velsar, Alkaban-AQ) for advanced prostate cancer treatment. At a meeting of the American Association for Cancer Research, the investigators reported that half the patients on this treatment showed a 50 percent or greater decline in the blood levels of the prostate-specific antigen (PSA), one way to monitor treatment success.

The length of chemotherapy treatment can vary depending on the drug, the extent of the cancer, and other factors. Some doctors are trying portable chemotherapy administration, in which a device that looks somewhat like a camera bag is worn. Tubes lead from the device to a vein and allow medication to travel throughout the body. It has the potential to lessen the time spent at a hospital or clinic for chemotherapy treatments, or to reduce the incidence of hospitalization.

Chemotherapy drugs act either by killing tumor cells or by preventing them from multiplying. One problem with chemotherapy, however, is that the drugs work not just on the cancer cells but on all rapidly dividing cells, even the normal ones. They can therefore have an undesirable effect on intestinal lining, bone marrow, and hair follicles, causing patients to experience nausea and vomiting, anemia and hair loss.

But in recent years, antinausea drugs have been developed that can reduce the problems of both nausea and vomiting. Hair loss is more difficult to combat. The best advice for most patients seems to be to anticipate it and remember that regrowth usually occurs fairly rapidly.

RADIATION THERAPY

Traditionally, patients whose prostate cancer has spread to the lymph nodes in the pelvis have not done well with *radiation therapy.* But researchers at Duke University suggested recently in *Urology* that this therapy might be worth a try in patients with whom a single microscopically positive node was found during the dissection of pelvic lymph nodes.

In reviewing the records of more than one hundred prostate cancer patients, the researchers found that those with a single positive node did well with radiation therapy. Those with more extensive metastases did not appear to be curable with radiation therapy. The researchers acknowledge that more study is needed before definite recommendations can be made.

For now, radiation therapy is sometimes recommended if prostate cancer has spread to the bones. It can help relieve the bone pain that often accompanies advanced prostate cancer.

BONE PAIN

Bone pain due to metastases is common, especially if the prostate cancer spreads to the spine and weight-bearing bones. It can be difficult to differentiate the pain of metastasis from the pain of arthritis. A bone scan and X rays can sometimes help determine the source of the pain.

Pain management can be a substantial problem for prostate cancer patients, reported Dr. Richard Payne of the University of Cincinnati at an American Cancer Society conference. In a survey of reports from oncology practices, he found that 55 to 100 percent of patients with prostate cancer complained of pain.

For advanced cases of prostate cancer in particular, pain control is an important part of treatment. As doctors are increasingly recognizing, the fear of pain is a major part of the anxiety occurring when cancer is diagnosed.

Pain is so complex that an entire specialty area of medicine is now devoted to it. How a person responds to and handles pain depends on a multitude of factors, including cultural and ethnic background. Pain associated with cancer can be acute, such as the type that often follows an operation, or it can be chronic, which is the case when a tumor grows and puts pressure on nerves.

If your pain is interfering with activity, ask your doctor what medication can be prescribed. Doctors usually begin by prescribing simple medicines such as aspirin, acetaminophen, and antiinflammatory drugs. If those do not work, stronger pain relievers such as codeine can be prescribed. Stronger narcotics such as morphine are usually reserved for the worst pain.

In addition to using medicines to control pain, you might want to consider massage or relaxation exercises. Anything you do to help yourself relax—admittedly not an easy task during an illness—may help reduce pain. Radiation therapy to a particular area of bone can very effectively relieve pain as well. If the pain is more diffuse, strontium administration can be helpful. In this technique, radioactive strontium is given and absorbed by the bones. The radiation is thus delivered to the whole skeleton, thereby providing pain relief.

Sometimes the prostate itself can enlarge and obstruct the flow of urine. If this happens, a transurethral resection of the prostate (TURP) may be necessary to unblock the bladder. (See Chapter 2 for more information on TURP.)

MONITORING TREATMENT

To track the progress of treatment, your doctor will probably order blood tests—either the prostate-specific antigen
(PSA) test, which you may have undergone to help diagnose the cancer—or the prostatic acid phosphatase (PAP)
test, which you may have undergone as well. In a study
published in the *Journal of Urology* comparing the two
tests, researchers in Quebec found the PSA test superior
to the PAP for predicting disease recurrence in stages C
and D cancer patients treated by combination endocrine
therapy.

How often you will return to your doctor for checkups
depends on a number of factors. The important thing is
not to miss a checkup. Enabling your doctor to monitor
your treatment so that any new symptoms can be evaluated is the best way to stay as healthy as possible.

For more information on staying healthy, see Chapter 9.

RECURRENCES

Although many of the remissions seen after beginning
hormonal therapy can last for years, most tumors will
eventually become active again.

---

*Even though some patients know their cancer can re-
turn, they say they can successfully put that fear out of
their minds once treatment seems to be working. Asked if
he worried about recurrence, one man answered without
hesitation: "I don't give it a thought." But he's not leaving
everything to luck. "I go in periodically for a checkup," he
said.*

SURVIVAL

Overall, men with advanced prostate cancer have a 29-percent five-year survival rate, according to the National Cancer Institute. Those diagnosed with cancer localized to the prostate have a 74-percent five-year survival rate. But these statistics are based on men diagnosed in 1974 through 1986, and today's treatments are better. Statistics, moreover, don't always tell the whole story. Each patient is an individual, and your doctor will prescribe the treatment best able to give you the best quality of life for the longest period of time.

SECOND OPINIONS

Before you consent to treatment, you might wish to obtain a second opinion. See the Appendix for more information about how to go about getting a second opinion.

CLINICAL TRIALS

If your doctor feels that experimental treatments, not yet approved, might help, it could be suggested that you consider undergoing investigational treatment as part of a clinical trial. To inform patients and doctors about available clinical trials, the National Cancer Institute has developed a data base called Physicians Data Query (PDQ) to give doctors information about which studies are accepting patients.

To access the system, doctors can use their own office computers, a facsimile machine, or a medical library computer system. Your doctor can call the NCI's Cancer Information Service, (800) 4-CANCER. (For more information on clinical trials, see the Appendix.)

CHAPTER·7

Investigational Treatments for Prostate Cancer

The treatment of prostate cancer has improved greatly in recent years, but there is still much progress to be made. Numerous research studies are under way to better understand prostate cancer and to develop more effective treatments. Some researchers are looking at new drugs and other investigational treatments. Others are studying combinations of established treatments to see if these combinations can improve the chances for survival. In addition, a growing understanding of why and how cancer spreads is leading to the development of techniques that might arrest or even prevent metastasis.

Some experts complain that prostate cancer research lags behind breast cancer research by ten years. But the picture is improving. In 1991, the National Cancer Institute budgeted $92.7 million for breast cancer research and $13.8 million for prostate cancer research. By 1992, the breast cancer research budget had grown to about $132.7 million and the prostate cancer research budget, while still well below that for breast cancer, had doubled to $27.6 million. In 1993, more than $28.5 million is projected for prostate cancer research; $136.7 million for breast cancer research.

Some of these investigational studies are described in the pages that follow. As you read these pages, other research could be under way or these investigations may be much farther along. To see if any of these studies might apply to you, consult your own physician, who has access to information about investigational treatments by contacting the National Cancer Institute via computer or facsimile machine. (For details on how to get patient information from the NCI's PDQ System and how to find out more about clinical trials, see the Appendix.)

Because prostate cancer is slow growing, it takes many years to assess the effectiveness of new treatments. It may take ten to fifteen years before the true worth of any new prostate cancer treatment can be determined conclusively. Unfortunately, the preliminary good results of some treatments are not always maintained over the long term.

The promise of a "quick cure" should arouse suspicion. Throughout history, there have always been questionable cancer cures, some out-and-out quackery. But you can learn to distinguish quackery from legitimate treatment. Some advice on how to do this can be found later in this chapter.

ENZYME-INHIBITING DRUGS

Someday it may be possible to treat prostate cancer by simply taking a drug to shrink the gland and the tumor. Some researchers say that the new drug finasteride (Proscar), discussed in Chapter 2 as a treatment for benign prostatic hypertrophy, may be an effective treatment for early-stage prostate cancer as well. But it is too soon to say. Merck, the drug's manufacturer, found finasteride ineffective in treating late-stage prostate cancer.

Finasteride works by blocking the enzyme that usually interacts with the hormone testosterone to produce dihydrotestosterone. It is dihydrotestosterone that stimulates the prostate gland to grow and enlarge in the condition called benign prostatic hypertrophy (BPH). But as yet, finasteride's usefulness in treating early-stage prostate cancer is unknown.

UPCOMING STUDIES

The National Cancer Institute plans to begin a study in which a single hormone therapy is compared with complete androgen blockade for treatment of recurrent prostate cancer following radical prostatectomy or radiation therapy. The rationale follows the double-up therapy approach sometimes used to treat breast cancer, according to Dr. Andrew Dorr of the NCI's Division of Cancer Treatment.

Also under study is a drug called suramin, used to treat African sleeping sickness. It could have merit in treating prostate cancer. Although experts speculate that it interferes with tumor growth factors, they do not know exactly how it works.

COMBINATION CHEMOTHERAPY

As noted on page 69 some researchers are trying a combination of the anticancer drugs estramustine phosphate sodium (Emcyt) and vinblastine sulfate (Velban, Velsar, Alkaban-AQ), according to a report in *Urology Times*. When this treatment approach was used in twenty-five patients, about half had a 50 percent or greater decrease in levels of prostate-specific antigen (PSA), an indication that the therapy was killing the tumor cells.

Patients reported nausea but in general tolerated the treatment well. Most of the men had previously undergone orchiectomy or external beam radiation therapy. Patients who need chemotherapy will probably be referred to an oncologist, who is aware of the latest treatment recommendations.

RADIATION AND HYPERTHERMIA

Other researchers are investigating a combination of hyperthermia with radiation treatment. Using hyperthermia to kill cancer cells is not a new idea. Temperatures exceeding about 106 degrees Fahrenheit (41 degrees C) will damage or kill cells preparing to divide and ones that are poorly oxygenated.

Since cancer cells are not always killed by radiation alone, some doctors think the combination of radiation and hyperthermia might be more effective, since heat seems to make the tumor cells more sensitive to radiation.

Hyperthermia can be delivered in a number of ways. The whole body can be heated or microwave applicators can be inserted into or close to the tumor. Writing in the journal *Urology*, Dr. Issac Kaver and his colleagues at the Medical College of Virginia reported a laboratory study combining radiation and heat treatment to kill prostate cancer cells. First the cells were exposed to radiation and then to temperatures of 43 degrees centigrade for one hour. The combination of therapies was a better cancer-cell killer than either of the two alone.

HIGH-ENERGY RADIATION THERAPY

Standard radiation therapy usually depends on the use of X rays or gamma rays. These kinds of rays have enough energy to reach and destroy deep-seated tumors.

A variation of radiation therapy employs accelerators that may use protons, helium ions, and neutrons. This type of radiation is called *high linear energy transfer radiation*. Some experts say this method kills cancer cells more effectively than standard therapy does, but it is available at only a handful of facilities in the country.

ONCOGENE THERAPY

Cancer researchers have discovered that some normal genes may somehow be changed into genes that promote cancer growth. These cancer-promoting genes are called *oncogenes*. (*Onco* is a Greek word meaning tumor, swelling, or mass.) Scientists also know that genes called *suppressor genes* normally but not always stop the formation of oncogenes.

This research opens up the exciting possibility of "gene therapy" in which the defective gene—the oncogene or a faulty suppressor gene—could be replaced. This research is in its infancy and use in patients is in the distant future. At a recent conference on prostate cancer, Stanford University researcher Donna Peehl reported that the role of gene therapy has not yet been established in the area of prostate cancer treatment.

BIOLOGICAL THERAPY

This therapeutic approach tries to get your body to fight cancer by using a variety of substances to boost, redirect, or reactivate your own natural defense against disease. These substances can be naturally occurring in the body or can be made in a laboratory.

A variety of such biological methods to treat cancer is under investigation. According to a recent report in the *Mayo Clinic Health Letter,* some researchers are experimenting with proteins called *interferons* and *interleukins,* which the body makes to fight infections. By injecting a synthetic version of these substances, it may be possible to stimulate the immune system to fight the cancer.

Substances called *colony-stimulating factors,* which boost production of white blood cells, may allow higher doses of chemotherapy to be used. Other researchers are studying the concept of removing T-cells—which recognize and attack cancer cells—boosting their growth, and then returning them to the body to fight the cancer. *Tumor necrosis factors* are proteins that destroy tumor cells. Research is being conducted on how to increase the production that naturally occurs in the body.

Substances called *monoclonal antibodies* are proteins made by the body to attack cancer cells. Researchers are trying to make "designer" monoclonal antibodies that kill specific types of cancer. When the designer antibodies attach themselves to tumor cells, they might help deliver medications and radiation to fight the specific cancer.

NEW UNDERSTANDING OF METASTASIS

Meanwhile, other researchers are investigating the process of metastasis—why and how a cancer spreads and what can stop it or prevent it from spreading. Since Dr. Joseph-Claude Récamier's 1829 treatise on the nature of metastasis, in which he showed that cancer cells from the originally diagnosed tumors could spread, researchers have been trying to better understand the process.

Recently, National Cancer Institute researchers have made some astounding discoveries about the spread of cancer. According to an extensive report in *Scientific American*, they are focusing on two areas: understanding how the genes inside a tumor cell enable it to spread, and finding out what happens at the cellular level that allows the invasion of cancer cells to occur.

They have identified substances called *metalloproteinases*, enzymes secreted by cancer cells that researchers speculate play a major role in metastasis. Researchers hope now to develop drugs to inhibit the production and action of these enzymes.

They can describe on a cellular level the steps a tumor cell goes through when it invades another tissue or organ. First, the tumor cell must adhere adequately to a cell membrane. Once the tumor cell adheres, destructive enzymes are activated. This clears the way, so to speak, for the tumor cells to enter. Researchers also believe that the suppressor genes can prevent these steps from occurring.

Other areas of research are focusing on what can be done, once the cancer has spread, to arrest its growth. Elise Kohn, a National Cancer Institute researcher, has recognized a new type of compound that might help arrest the growth of prostate and other cancers. These compounds, called *carboxyamide aminoimidazoles* (CAIs), have stopped the growth of prostate cancers and other tumors in laboratory experiments. Now the researchers plan to study CAIs in humans. Although these studies are in very early phases, scientists say they look promising.

AVOIDING "QUACK" CURES

Unorthodox treatment methods for cancer abound. Pick up a supermarket tabloid, and it seems that a cancer "breakthrough" is reported every other week.

According to the American Cancer Society, patients' use of questionable or unproven cancer treatments is a growing phenomenon. A 1984 report from a congressional committee found that patients spent about $4 billion annually on unproven cancer cures. The Cancer Society estimates even more is spent today, partly the result of lobbying efforts from "alternative therapy" groups.

Who seeks such treatment? According to ACS research, victims of quackery are found in every socioeconomic level. Nor are they necessarily those classified as terminal or beyond the hope of cure. Up to half of cancer patients either consider or use unorthodox treatments, according to Dr. Barrie R. Cassileth of the University of Pennsylvania Cancer Center and Helene Brown of the Jonsson Comprehensive Cancer Center at UCLA, who wrote the booklet "Questionable Cancer Medicine," published by the American Cancer Society. Contrary to what you might think, many who offer the questionable treatments are licensed M.D.'s. The authors found that 51 percent of 166 unorthodox cancer practitioners were M.D.'s. Of those, 18 percent were board certified in different specialties.

While "cures" vary from year to year, here are some of the most commonly promoted alternative therapies.

- **Metabolic Therapy.** This treatment usually includes special diets, a cleansing "detoxification" of the body, and perhaps high-dose vitamins and minerals. This therapy is based on the idea that toxins and waste materials in the body interfere with healing. Often, an advocate of metabolic therapy will suggest colonic irrigation or enemas. Mainstream experts warn that deaths have been reported from such colonic irrigation. Special macrobiotic regimens can cause nutritional deficiency, known to be particularly hazardous for cancer patients.

- **Mental Attitude Therapy.** This treatment approach has a "do-it-yourself" quality suggesting that self-management of stress and other life-style changes alone might alter the disease course. Some treatment approaches involve mental imagery in which the patient visualizes the destruction of cancer cells. Many mainstream medical providers, acknowledging a growing acceptance of a mind/body link in health and disease, see nothing harmful about such techniques as mental imagery and stress reduction, but they caution that these techniques are meant to supplement, not replace, conventional medical therapy.

Unconventional Treatment Approaches Through the Years

Here are some examples of unorthodox approaches to cancer treatment touted through the years:

Thomsonianism—a theory advanced in the early to mid 1800s that said disease springs from a general cause and is cured by a general remedy. Hot baths are one example of a cure-all remedy.

Homeopathy—a system of therapy especially popular from 1850 until the turn of the century, based on administration of tiny doses of many different drugs. This therapeutic system, which some say is making a comeback today, includes more than three thousand different drugs.

Naturopathy—the belief that disease results from violation of the natural laws of living. The best cures are "natural," such as special diets or colonic irrigation. This approach was especially popular in the 1890s.

Other Cancer "Cures": Since the turn of the century, a variety of special unorthodox cancer "cures" have been touted, ranging from laetrile to megadoses of vitamins to psychic treatments.

Source: "Questionable Cancer Medicine," the American Cancer Society.

It is understandable that cancer patients who have not done well with conventional therapy want to pursue every promising lead, but a *caveat emptor* attitude is essential. When you hear of new treatments, differentiate between anecdotal information and scientific evidence.

Before a treatment can be government approved, researchers must conduct scientific studies with large numbers of people. They must compare the "treatment group" to the "no treatment (placebo) group" and to other, established treatments. They must prove it works in a significant number of cases and that its benefits outweigh its complications.

Be wary of cures that are touted as "secret." If a "miracle treatment" is available only from one or two practitioners, watch out. Be wary, too, if the cost is high. When you hear of a treatment that is new and sounds too good to be true, it probably is. Consider asking some of the questions listed in the following table.

Questions to Ask about New Cancer Therapies or Studies

---

1. Is the study sponsored or funded by the National Cancer Institute, the American Cancer Society, a well-known pharmaceutical company, or a respected hospital or cancer center?

2. Does the study include control-group patients? Is it based on scientific theory?

3. Have the patients receiving the treatment been followed up? For how long? What are the results?

4. Who is conducting the study? What are the leader's credentials and training? Is the investigator affiliated with a teaching hospital or a reputable cancer center or university?

5. Have any data been published on the treatment and how it works in the laboratory, in animal studies, and in human trials?

If you hear of an investigational treatment that sounds legitimate and think it might help, ask your doctor about it. Your doctor will know if you fit the protocol and if the treatment might help you.

CHAPTER · 8

The Emotional Side of Prostate Cancer

Eight men walked into a meeting room filled with over-stuffed couches and chairs. At first, they shifted in their seats and gazed at the floor, their hands, or the ceiling. Slowly, with the help of a leader, they began to speak.

One talked about his fear of dying when he learned he had prostate cancer. Another confided that he worried most about the effect on his marriage. What if he should never again be capable of having sex with his wife? A third admitted that he was angry, very angry.

One man could not decide which of two possible treatments to undergo and had come to the meeting hoping someone could share his experience. All of them had to admit that a diagnosis of prostate cancer makes it impossible to ignore their own mortality.

Across the country, there are growing numbers of such "support groups" for prostate cancer patients. Many doctors are suggesting that patients investigate stress-reduction classes and other ways to allay anxiety. Some men with prostate cancer are learning what women with breast cancer have known for many years: The problem isn't purely physical.

"Prostate cancer is a disease with a lot of emotional involvement," said Lucius, a fifty-six-year-old artist who underwent a radical prostatectomy a month after he learned he had cancer. He still remembers his "death dreams." "I would dream of crashing into a black hearse," he recalled.

A discussion of the psychological ramifications of prostate cancer was even on the agenda at a recent annual meeting of the American Urological Association. Doctors say the diagnosis of prostate cancer can have a devastating effect on a patient's ability to communicate with his own family, friends, and his doctor.

No one can generalize about an individual's reaction to a cancer diagnosis, but in addition to fearing death, most men diagnosed with prostate cancer worry about the possible effects on sexual desire and the ability to get an erection. Men also worry about the possible side effects of treatment, especially urinary incontinence. And some men, if they are not yet retired, have to get used to the fact that, at least temporarily, they may give up their provider or coprovider role within the family.

SUPPORT GROUP "HOW-TOS"

Growing numbers of doctors believe that a support group can help reopen these lines of communication so that men can sort out their feelings—but men must be willing to give it a try. In fact, the American Urological Association now distributes to interested physician members a "how-to" manual on establishing support groups. If your physician decides to help start such a group, he or she may send out a letter to patients with diagnosed prostate cancer, with an invitation for them to come to an organizational meeting. The initial meeting is often held at a hospital, but can be held at other facilities. Some men prefer other environments where they can relax more easily. Most of these meetings last an hour or an hour and a half. The physician may attend the first meeting or the first few, and then participate only in an advisory role. Often, these groups invite guest speakers, such as a psychologist or a surgeon, to explain treatment and other concerns.

If your physician does not know of a support group, check with your local American Cancer Society office and/or local hospitals. Some hospitals offer support groups or courses aimed at helping to meet the psychological needs of cancer patients. The sessions typically include stress reduction, deep inner relaxation, and development of mental imagery. The goal is to help prostate cancer patients develop coping skills to deal with treatment, stress, and fears.

In some states, another option is the Wellness Community, a ten-year-old network of support groups and other services for cancer patients. The community, begun by a Beverly Hills attorney turned social psychologist, attracted nationwide attention a few years ago when the late performer Gilda Radner, diagnosed with ovarian cancer, attended meetings at the headquarters community in Santa Monica, California. At these Wellness Communities, patients are not charged for access to support groups led by licensed psychotherapists and classes in relaxation, guided imagery, and stress reduction.

The program founder, Dr. Harold Benjamin, encourages patients to take an active part in their treatment—to become what he calls "patient actives." Some other programs have adopted his orientation. No one is saying that an active stance will guarantee a cure or even a longer life, but some advocates contend that taking an active role in treatment decisions and stress reduction can enhance the patient's "quality of life."

(For more information on support groups, see the Appendix.)

One effect of dealing with the psychological fallout of cancer, experts say, is that patients tend to question their doctors more aggressively, asking for more details about treatment than other patients might. Experts observe that active patients rarely walk away from established medical care. In fact, support group members are likely to persuade disenchanted fellow group members to finish recommended medical treatment regimens. While not everyone believes in the "emotional" side of cancer, growing numbers of research studies support this mind/body link —the premise that your emotional state affects your physical healing, or that a positive attitude might help you feel better, both physically and emotionally.

WHAT THE STUDIES FIND

Here is a sampling of recent studies exploring the mind/body link in cancer patients and their families.

One study reported in *The Lancet* compared women with advanced breast cancer who attended weekly group meetings for a year with those cancer patients who did not go to support group meetings. All patients had routine cancer care. Those who attended support group meetings were also offered self-hypnosis for pain. On average, the women who attended the weekly meetings lived twice as long as those who did not, says Dr. David Spiegel of the Stanford University School of Medicine, the lead researcher. The support group patients lived an average of thirty-six months from the time they began to attend the meetings; those who didn't attend averaged eighteen months of survival after the study began.

A UCLA study evaluated the effects of group intervention in patients who had undergone surgery for malignant melanoma, a virulent skin cancer. Patients who attended group sessions learned problem-solving skills, stress management in the form of relaxation techniques, and received psychological support.

At the six-month follow-up, the patients who went to group sessions had more vigor and more effective coping skills than patients who did not attend the sessions. The patients who went to the group sessions also tended to be less depressed, less fatigued, and less moody. The study is reported by UCLA researcher Fawzy I. Fawzy and his team in the *Archives of General Psychiatry*.

In another recent study, researchers Thomas G. Burish and Richard A. Jenkins at Vanderbilt University found that relaxation therapy can help cancer patients cope with chemotherapy. Reporting their findings in the journal *Health Psychology*, the researchers compared the effectiveness of *biofeedback* training and relaxation therapy in reducing negative reactions to chemotherapy.

With biofeedback therapy, patients learned how to control muscle tension and skin temperature. Heightened skin temperature and increased muscle tension often precede nausea. The relaxation-therapy patients learned how to relax their muscles in a progressive manner and to use imagery to help themselves remain calm. The relaxation therapy was found to be better than the biofeedback in helping control undesirable side effects.

People cope in many different ways when they are trying to come to grips with a diagnosis of cancer. In a recent study published in the journal *Health Psychology*, researchers found five different coping choices were made among a sample of 603 cancer patients. There were those patients who sought social support, those who focused on the positive, those who distanced themselves from the diagnosis, those who used avoidance techniques such as praying or fantasizing, and those who used avoidance techniques such as becoming reclusive.

The researchers, led by Christine Dunkel-Schetter from UCLA, found that most people used a variety of coping methods, not just one. The researchers found that coping by "distancing" was by far the most commonly used technique. When patients used this method, they tended to make light of their diagnosis or tried to forget the whole thing. They used healthier "distancing" techniques too. Some, for instance, began to treat the illness as a challenge.

Other research suggests that some cancer patients seem to need group support more than others. Patients who have what researchers call "good ego strength" and have had a strong sense of control over their lives before their cancer diagnosis often exhibit those same strengths in dealing with the diagnosis. This was the conclusion of a research team led by Linda Edgar of McGill University, in a study of more than two hundred patients published in the journal *Cancer*. The patients with lower ego strength were more likely to need more intervention.

Patients who choose to cope by joining a support group

should be aware that these same researchers found the best time to join might not be immediately after diagnosis. Edgar's team compared the coping of patients receiving psychological support immediately after the diagnosis with those receiving support four months after the diagnosis. The best time to seek out a group, if that option is appealing, seems to be several months after learning of the diagnosis.

Support groups can also help spouses of cancer patients, another study suggests. University of Iowa psychologists Robert S. Baron and Carolyn E. Cutrona and their research team interviewed spouses of thirty men and women whose spouses had cancers of the kidney, prostate, or other urological areas. Then they took blood tests of the spouses. Those spouses who reported they had high levels of moral support from friends to get through the crisis had better immune functioning. The study is reported in the *Journal of Personality and Social Psychology*. The researchers say they cannot explain the precise mechanism or mechanisms responsible for this finding, but they believe the association seems strong enough to encourage further research.

WHAT THE PATIENTS SAY

Patients say a support group helps them in many ways. It gets them out of the house and helps them interact with people. Some report that it is helpful to be in contact with others who can identify with how they feel. Some men say participating in such group discussions helps bring them out of themselves, out of their own problems and depression.

Louis, 68, has been going to a regular support group meeting for about six months. "I feel good in a group like this," he says. "We talk about different things we have in common. We share common difficulties. I have my moments of being depressed. Then I stop to think. I pick myself up. And I think some of these guys are a lot worse off than me. Sometimes I can say something to help them, and that makes me feel good."

Added John: "There is a certain camaraderie. . . . The members become a family for you. They know what you are going through, much more than your family. Most important," he said, "you can see other people fighting cancer and surviving. From the media, what you get mostly are the death notices."

CHAPTER · 9

Staying Healthy

More than seven million Americans alive today have had cancer, according to the American Cancer Society. And many of them have had prostate cancer.

Survival rates have inched up impressively since the turn of the century, when few cancer patients had any hope of long-term survival. In the 1930s, fewer than one in five patients was alive at least five years after treatment, according to the American Cancer Society. In the 1960s it rose to one in three. Today, about four of every ten patients who get cancer will be alive five years after the diagnosis, according to the Society. Of course, for prostate cancer, the prognosis is much better. The earlier the diagnosis, the better the outlook. But even if your cancer was caught in the early stages and your doctor has assured you that your outlook is good, it is natural to be somewhat anxious about relapse or cancer spread.

Lucius, a fifty-six-year-old artist who underwent surgery for prostate cancer, put it this way: "Once you've had cancer . . . anytime you feel a glitch in your body, you worry." Yet, he allows, he can't let that anxiety consume his life. In general, his outlook is: "Life is grand."

One approach to allay anxiety is to be vigilant, and when symptoms develop report them promptly to your doctor. You should also follow to the letter your doctor's recommendations about the frequency of checkups. Last but not least, take good care of yourself on a daily basis through sound diet and exercise.

If your cancer was not detected until the later stages, the chances of controlling the disease are improving every day. For you, the concern may be how to live pain free and to make good use of your time. Your doctor will help you with this.

CHECKUP SCHEDULE

How often you return for a medical checkup depends on a number of factors. Your doctor is the best one to recommend the schedule that best suits your own individual needs. In general, men who have undergone a radical prostatectomy should return for a prostate-specific antigen (PSA) test every three to four months for the first two years and then every six months, or even annually.

Checkups for men who have undergone hormone therapy, radiation therapy, or combination therapy usually follow a similar schedule. Exactly how long you go between checkups depends on your doctor's recommendations and how well you do at each checkup.

RELAPSE

If your cancer does recur, there are many options. Your doctor may recommend radiation therapy, hormone therapy, or chemotherapy. These treatments can be effective in locally recurrent cancer or metastatic cancer.

In a study of twenty-four patients with recurrences after prostatectomy, 74 percent had tumor control after radiation therapy, reported Dr. Carlos A. Perez of Washington University at an American Cancer Society conference. And 70 percent of those survived relapse-free five years after treatment.

Radiation can also help with the pain that accompanies metastasis to the bone. More than half the patients reported complete relief, according to Washington University studies, and about a third got at least partial relief from bone pain after radiation therapy.

CANCER PREVENTION AND EARLY DETECTION

It is wise for everyone, former cancer patient or not, to have an overall knowledge of cancer prevention. One important measure is to undergo periodic examinations for cancer. The following is the checkup schedule for men recommended by the American Cancer Society.

Checkup Recommendations

Test or Procedure	Age	How Often/Type Cancer Detected
Sigmoidoscopy*	Over 50	Every 3–5 years based on doctor's advice; colon cancer
Stool test for blood	Over 50	Every year; stomach, intestine, colon cancers
Digital rectal exam	Over 40	Every year; colon, prostate cancers
PSA	Over 50	Every year; prostate cancers
General Cancer Checkup**	Over 40	Every year

*Sigmoidoscopy is the examination of the rectum and sigmoid colon with a special viewing instrument, the sigmoidoscope.
**For men, this cancer checkup should include examination for cancers of the thyroid, testicles, prostate, lymph nodes, mouth, and skin.
Source: American Cancer Society

There are several commonsense measures that minimize cancer risk. Cigarette smoking accounts for about 85 percent of lung cancer cases among men (75 percent among women), according to the American Cancer Society. Minimizing the negative effect of sunlight by using sun block can cut risk of skin cancer; minimizing exposure to industrial agents like asbestos and nickel can reduce cancer risk as well. A prudent, low-fat diet is believed to cut the risk of several kinds of cancer. Heavy alcohol intake leads to more cancers of the mouth and throat, among other sites.

It's also wise to know what the American Cancer Society calls the seven early warning signs of cancer. They include:

- a change in bowel or bladder habits
- a sore that does not heal
- unusual discharge or bleeding
- a thickening or lump in the breast or elsewhere
- indigestion or difficulty in swallowing
- obvious change in a wart or mole
- nagging cough or hoarseness.

Since there are often no early warning signs for prostate cancer, the best preventive course is to undergo an annual digital rectal exam and other tests recommended by your physician.

IMPROVING QUALITY OF LIFE AFTER CANCER

While medical researchers focus on the best treatments for prostate cancer, other experts are focusing on improving what they call "quality of life" for cancer patients. The concern of these researchers and clinicians—psychologists, psychiatrists, social workers, family therapists—is to keep the life of the patient and his loved ones as enjoyable and productive as possible.

Some doctors encourage their prostate cancer patients to participate in a few counseling sessions after they hear the diagnosis, so that they can be helped to sort out their feelings.

There is also a growing awareness among counseling professionals that prostate cancer affects not just the patient, but the entire family. It is not unusual for patients and their spouses or other family members to seek out some counseling together. They may be concerned about a range of issues, including such practical matters as getting along without one paycheck for a while or combating appetite loss, or more intimate matters such as sexual functioning.

EXERCISE

Your doctor may suggest you take up, or resume, an exercise program once you feel well enough and your medical condition has stabilized. Those who have never exercised might need some convincing about the benefits of physical activity. In general, the better physical shape you are in, the better you can tolerate any cancer treatment.

Exercise might help you recover faster after an operation. In addition, you will reap all the other benefits of exercise: it helps control weight, reduces stress, lowers your blood pressure, and keeps your cholesterol level low, to name a few.

The most suitable exercise program depends on your condition, of course, along with your body weight and your previous exercise habits. Consider enlisting the help of an exercise physiologist or a physical therapist at your community hospital. There are many exercise videos that you can pop into your VCR and follow in the privacy of your own home. Not all of these are excessively vigorous programs. Some are designed especially for beginners, senior citizens, or disabled persons.

NUTRITION

If you never paid much attention to nutrition before, this is a good time to develop new habits. By eating wisely, you might help the effectiveness of your treatment and speed healing. You will certainly feel better on a sound diet than on one filled with junk food and excessive fat.

If you think you need help in your nutritional strategies, ask your doctor to refer you to a registered dietitian who is specially trained to help you develop and maintain a sound nutrition program. In a session or two, the dietitian will probably be able to develop an individualized menu plan tailored to your needs. Or the hospital may provide nutritional counseling before your discharge.

You may experience loss of appetite during chemotherapy or radiation treatments or due to simple fear and anxiety. Sometimes chemotherapy or radiation will distort your sense of smell and taste. Certain foods may just not taste good. In this case, you might ask a nutritionist which foods to substitute in order to ensure getting the right combination of nutrients.

If you can't eat a full meal and are worried about excess weight loss, there are a number of other things you could do to ensure you get enough calories. Try to snack between meals, eating calorie-laden foods like milk shakes, if they're not forbidden by your doctor. Exercising on a regular basis might improve your appetite, and making mealtimes pleasant and relaxing may help you eat more, too. If none of this works, your doctor might prescribe medication to boost your appetite.

Once your appetite is back to normal, you should consider improving your diet in line with government guidelines for cancer prevention. In brief, that means eating a low-fat, high-fiber diet with moderate or no alcohol intake.

Eat plenty of fresh fruits and raw vegetables and minimize consumption of fatty meats.

Some researchers claim that certain minerals and vitamins can minimize cancer risk. Selenium, for instance, is a trace element needed by the body in tiny amounts to preserve elasticity of body tissues and improve oxygen supply to the heart.

Selenium is found in meats, vegetables, and dairy products. Don't increase your selenium intake, either by supplements or diet, without consulting your doctor.

The mineral zinc has also been linked with prostate health. Zinc is found in wheat bran, wheat germ, animal meats, and seafoods. Again, it's not a good idea to decide on your own what amount of zinc you need. Ask your doctor or a nutritionist.

SEXUAL REHABILITATION

Many men with prostate cancer worry about their sexual functioning after treatment. For men with localized disease, the outlook has been improving in recent years. Numbers vary from study to study, but external beam radiation can leave 25 to 50 percent of men with new erection problems, according to a report from the Cleveland Clinic Foundation presented at an American Cancer Society conference.

Implanted radiation usually causes less damage to erectile function. "Nerve-sparing" radical prostatectomy, if it can adequately remove all the cancer, has improved the recovery of men's erectile functioning as well.

Studies show that men are more likely to recover full potency if they are under age fifty, and if their tumors are smaller and both neurovascular bundles can be spared. After local treatment, many men report that sexual desire and the ability to experience orgasm remain, even though erections may not be as rigid.

Men who have undergone one of the forms of hormonal therapy are less likely to regain or retain potency. In addition, they often report an impairment or absence of sexual desire.

John, 58, a technician, was put on hormone therapy and soon developed potency problems. "I've been finding out what good old testosterone has been doing all these years," he says. He differentiates between attraction and arousal toward the opposite sex. He can still feel attracted, he said, but his feelings do not "cross the line" to the point of arousal.

Some men might wish to explore routes to "sexual rehabilitation." One way might be to participate in sex therapy, designed to enhance communication between a man and his partner.

The ability to obtain an erection can be restored by a number of methods. One way is to take oral medication that stimulates blood flow into the penis. If that does not work sufficiently, vacuum-assisted erection devices can help many patients, especially those who get a partial erection, to complete and maintain the erection.

There is a very high rate of patient and partner satisfaction with these devices. More than 90 percent of patients and their partners are satisfied with their use, and there are few if any complications associated with them. The devices are usually accompanied by an educational videotape and the manufacturers often maintain toll-free telephone numbers to answer consumer questions. Another option is learning to self-inject erection-causing medication directly into the penis.

If the medicines and devices do not work, permanently implanted penile prostheses can be considered. There are several models to choose from. The simplest and least likely to malfunction is called a "semirigid" device. Others work on a kind of hydraulic system and are inflated when an erection is desired. Only a minority of men need to resort to the implanted prostheses to maintain an erection. Most are happy with the vacuum devices. Your urologist will be able to give you more information about all these options. Some experts recommend that all men receive an opportunity for sexual counseling after treatment for prostate cancer regardless of their age or whether they are currently involved in a romantic relationship. In such counseling sessions, therapists can also elaborate about ways other than intercourse in which a couple can express love and affection.

Some men say they simply accept the fact that their sex life is not what it used to be—but that they are grateful to be alive and that they have developed or maintained satisfying, if platonic, relationships.

Conclusion

As this book goes to press, other promising treatments for benign prostatic hypertrophy and prostate cancer are under study. Remember, new techniques and operations discussed in this book may be even farther along than described. Consult your doctor, the American Cancer Society, or your local medical society for an update on diagnosis and treatment.

Whether you are treated for benign prostatic hypertrophy or prostate cancer, it is vital to remember to undergo preventive checkups. In coming years, doctors expect to improve their ability to diagnose prostate cancer, or recurring cancer, in its very earliest—and most curable—stages.

Glossary

anesthesia: use of drugs to reduce pain. Spinal anesthesia is injected into the spinal canal to block pain sensations. General ("whole body") anesthesia is given by injection, inhalation, or both. General anesthesia induces loss of consciousness and loss of sensation. Local anesthesia is given by injection. It induces loss of sensation in and around the body part to be treated.

anesthesiologist: medical doctor with special training in anesthesiology.

acute urinary retention: condition in which bladder is completely blocked; a catheter may be inserted to drain urine.

5-alpha reductase: the enzyme that normally converts the male hormone testosterone to dihydrotestosterone, the substance that stimulates unwanted growth of the prostate gland.

antiandrogens: hormone treatment used for

advanced prostate cancer; works by inhibiting the action of testosterone on prostate cancer cells.

autologous blood collection: donation of one's own blood for storage and possible later transfusion use.

benign prostatic hypertrophy: noncancerous enlargement of the prostate gland that typically begins around age forty.

biofeedback: technique in which a person uses information about a normally unconscious body function, like heart rate, to gain voluntary control over the function. The patient is connected to a recording instrument that measures heart rate and other parameters and alerts the patient to changes in those functions. After some experience, the patient learns how to use the information, or feedback, to change and control the body functions.

biological therapy: experimental cancer treatment based on boosting the body's ability to fight cancer. Among biological therapy substances under study: interferons and interleukins (proteins that the body makes to fight infections) and colony-stimulating factor (a substance that boosts white blood cell production).

biopsy: examination of tissue sample for cancer cells.

bone scan: test to help detect cancer spread to the bones; also used to measure density of bone tissue. A small amount of a radioactive substance is injected and collects in areas of abnormal bone activity.

brachytherapy: type of radiation therapy given by implantation of pellets of radioactive material. Also called implanted radiation or interstitial radiation.

cancer: abnormal and unrestrained cell growth in a tissue or organ.

carboxyamide aminoimidazoles (CAIs): compounds under study that have stopped prostate cancer growth in laboratory experiments.

carcinogens: cancer-causing agents.

chemotherapy: use of chemicals or drugs designed to kill or suppress cancer cells. Two examples are 5-fluorouracil and doxorubicin.

clinical trials: studies of experimental treatments, supported by the National Cancer Institute and other facilities throughout the United States and by similar institutions worldwide. Clinical trials are designed to answer scientific questions and evaluate whether a new treatment, already studied in the laboratory and in animals, is safe and effective for humans.

CT or CAT scan: series of X rays taken as a scanner revolves around the patient. The image creates a cross-sectional picture of the body area being scanned.

cystoscopy: examination of the urinary tract, done with a special viewing tube, to help pinpoint bladder obstruction.

Depolupron—see *leuprolide.*

diethylstilbestrol (DES): synthetic form of estrogen used to treat advanced prostate cancer, rarely used today.

To Bro. Richard

Date 6/10 Time G53 □ A.M. P.M.

WHILE YOU WERE OUT

From GINA

of

Phone 708 327 2103
Area Code   Number   Ext.

Fax
Area Code   Number

	Telephoned		Please call
	Came to see you	✓	Wants to see you

□ URGENT

Kevin 327-2102

WHILE YOU WERE OUT

To **Bro. RICHARD**

Date **6/7** Time **320** A.M. P.M.

From **Dr. Rob Hannigan's**

of **office**

Phone **708 - 216 - 5112**
Area Code — Number — Ext.

Fax _____
Area Code — Number

URGENT ☐

| Returned your call | Will call again |

Message *Call by 4:30 on*

on Monday

Kathy Mackazie

Signed *Margaret*

Quill Corporation • Re-order Number 7-92001

1062268

Message — To set appointment
for PSA Court.

Signed _____ Margaret

digital rectal exam: examination to help check for enlargement of the prostate gland and for prostate cancer. By inserting a gloved finger into the rectum, the doctor can feel the prostate gland through the rectal wall and detect abnormalities and enlargement.

doxorubicin: a kind of chemotherapy drug.

Emcyt: see *estramustine phosphate sodium*.

estramustine phosphate sodium (Emcyt): a kind of chemotherapy treatment used for advanced prostate cancer.

estrogen: female hormone therapy used in the past to treat advanced prostate cancer.

external beam radiation: radiation therapy given externally to kill cancer cells; for prostate cancer, usually given five days a week for six or seven weeks.

Eulexin: see *flutamide*.

finasteride (Proscar): newly released and approved drug that works by shrinking the prostate; used to treat enlargement of the prostate.

flow cytometry: procedure to measure biopsied cells' ability to give off light (fluorescence) and thus determine the amount of DNA (genetic material) within; helps doctors plan treatment.

fluorouracil (5-FU): chemotherapy drug used to treat advanced prostate cancer.

flutamide (Eulexin): hormone therapy used to treat advanced prostate cancer.

goserelin (Zoladex): medication known as an LHRH agonist used to treat advanced prostate cancer.

high-energy radiation therapy: variation of radiation therapy; employs accelerators that may use protons, helium ions, and neutrons to deliver radiation.

homeopathy: system of therapy, considered questionable by conventional health-care professionals, based on administration of tiny doses of drugs that in healthy people would produce symptoms of the disease treated.

hormone therapy: treatment involving use of hormones. For prostate cancer, female hormones are given to reduce or eliminate the production of testosterone, which prostate cancer cells need to grow.

hyperthermia: the use of heat therapy to shrink cancer cells. The entire body can be heated or microwave applicators can be inserted into the tumor.

Hytrin: see *terazosin*.

impotence: inability to achieve and maintain an erection.

incontinence: inability to control evacuative functions.

informed consent: permission given by patients allowing doctors to perform surgery or administer other treatments, based on an understanding by the patient of the risks and potential benefits.

interstitial (implanted) radiation: kind of radiation therapy given by implantation of pellets of radioactive material that delivers radiation directly to the cancer cells. About fifty pellets or seeds are implanted in the prostate, usually via an incision.

intravenous pyelography (IVP): procedure for obtaining X-ray pictures of the urinary system.

laparoscopic lymphadenectomy (LALA): procedure in which a telescopelike device (laparoscope) is inserted through a small opening in the abdomen and used to guide sampling of lymph nodes.

leuprolide (Lupron, Depolupron): a type of LHRH agonist; used to treat prostate cancer and, rarely, symptoms of benign prostatic hypertrophy.

LHRH agonists: drugs that suppress testosterone production (LHRH stands for luteinizing hormone-releasing hormone) and that are released from the brain and control the production of male and female sex hormones.

Lupron: see *leuprolide*.

lymph nodes: part of the body's lymphatic system; lymph nodes are found all over the body, but are concentrated in the neck, armpit, and groin. Lymph nodes are usually the first site of prostate cancer spread.

mental attitude therapy: cancer treatment considered questionable by conventional health-care providers; suggests self-management of stress and other life-style changes alone might alter the course of cancer and other diseases. Not to be confused with approaches in which stress reduction and other mental-change therapies are used in conjunction with traditional treatment.

metabolic therapy: unconventional cancer therapy

that involves special diets and "detoxification" of the body along with high-dose vitamins and minerals. Considered dangerous by conventional health professionals.

metalloproteinases: newly discovered enzymes secreted by cancer cells that researchers say may play a major role in the spread of cancer.

metastasis: spread of cancer.

microwave treatment: the use of heat to treat enlargement of the prostate gland.

mind/body link: belief that mental attitude and emotional state can affect physical healing, with a positive attitude helping patients feel better physically and emotionally.

Minipress: see *prazosin*.

nafarelin acetate (Synarel): a drug used to treat symptoms of benign prostatic hypertrophy and prostate cancer.

naturopathy: belief that disease results from violation of "natural" laws. The best cures, according to this philosophy, are natural. Considered a questionable therapy approach by conventional health-care providers.

nurse-anesthetist: nurse who has completed nursing school, critical-care nursing, and postgraduate study in anesthesia; also called a certified registered nurse-anesthetist or CRNA.

oncogene therapy: potential future cancer therapy in which a defective gene is replaced with a healthy new one.

oncogenes: special genes that control cell growth and division. When oncogenes are transformed by cancer-causing agents (carcinogens), cancer develops.

open prostatectomy: removal of the core of the prostate gland via an incision in the lower abdomen.

orchiectomy: operation to remove the testes; oldest form of hormone treatment for prostate cancer.

pelvic lymphadenectomy: sampling of lymph nodes around the prostate gland, usually done before a surgeon removes the gland. If cancer has spread to the lymph nodes, the surgeon will probably not remove the gland, because that would then offer little likelihood of cure.

penile prostheses: devices to help men achieve and maintain erections.

postvoid residual: the amount of urine left in the bladder after urinating; used to evaluate the severity of the enlargement of the prostate.

potency-sparing technique: a variation of the radical retropubic prostatectomy, in which the nerve bundles and blood vessels responsible for achieving and maintaining an erection are left in place. This operation is not usually feasible if the tumor is large or if the cancer is found on both sides of the prostate.

prazosin (Minipress): high-blood-pressure medicine; also prescribed to relieve symptoms of benign prostatic hypertrophy.

Proscar: see *finasteride*.

prostate gland: a solid, walnut-shaped organ situated in front of the rectum and just below the bladder. Its main function is to produce seminal fluid.

prostate-specific antigen (PSA) test: a procedure that measures blood levels of PSA, a protein secreted by the prostate. Elevated levels sometimes, but not always, indicate cancer.

prostatic acid phosphatase test (PAP): blood test to detect levels of prostatic acid phosphatase, an enzyme that can become elevated in the presence of prostate cancer. The newer prostate-specific antigen (PSA) test is more sensitive and has largely replaced the PAP test.

prostatitis: inflammation of the prostate gland.

radiation therapy: treatment involving the application of high-energy particles to destroy cancer in the tissues. Radiation therapy can be given via external beam or implanted pellets (interstitial radiation).

radical perineal prostatectomy: operation in which an incision is made between the scrotum and anus, allowing the surgeon to remove the prostate gland and surrounding tissues; requires about half the operating time of the radical retropubic prostatectomy.

radical prostatectomy: removal of the entire prostate gland and surrounding tissues.

radical retropubic prostatectomy: type of prostatectomy in which the incision runs from below the navel to the pubic bone or horizontally across the lower abdomen; entire prostate gland and lymph nodes are removed.

retrograde ejaculation: condition in which sperm goes backward into the bladder rather than being propelled out from the penis; a side effect of some prostate operations. It is not dangerous.

selenium: trace element needed by the body in tiny amounts; helps preserve elasticity of body tissues and improves the oxygen supply to the heart. Selenium is found in meat, fish, whole grains, and dairy products.

sigmoidoscopy: examination of the rectum and sigmoid colon with a special viewing instrument called a sigmoidoscope to check for any abnormalities.

staging systems: classifications used to describe cancer spread. One staging system classifies cancers from stages A through D (A for the smallest, least invasive cancers). Another is called the TNM system (T for tumor size; N for spread to lymph nodes; M for presence of metastasis).

stent: tiny tubular device, usually inserted permanently into the urethra to relieve prostate gland obstruction.

stricture: narrowing of a duct, canal, or other body passage.

strontium: a radioactive substance given to relieve the bone pain that can accompany advanced prostate cancer.

Synarel: see *nafarelin acetate.*

terazosin (Hytrin): High-blood-pressure medicine also used to treat the symptoms of benign prostatic hypertrophy.

testosterone: male sex hormone produced by the testes.

Thomsonianism: theory that disease springs from a general cause and is remedied by a "cure-all" such as a hot bath.

trabeculation: visible changes in the bladder wall, seen during cystoscopy, indicating changes in the urinary tract that can be due to obstruction.

transrectal ultrasound: test in which an instrument is inserted into the rectum, Sound waves are directed toward the prostate and bounce off it; a computer converts the sound-wave echoes into an image and printout to detect abnormal areas.

transurethral dilation of the prostate: procedure for benign prostatic hypertrophy; also called balloon dilation. Involves insertion of a catheter with a deflated balloon tip. Balloon is inflated to enlarge passage for urine flow.

transurethral incision of the prostate (TUIP): procedure in which an instrument is passed through the penis to make a cut in the prostate to relieve obstruction in benign prostatic hypertrophy.

transurethral resection of the prostate (TURP): operation in which the innermost core of the gland is removed, relieving compression on the urethra caused by benign prostatic hypertrophy.

transurethral ultrasound-guided laser-induced prostatectomy (TULIP): the use of laser to reduce tissue in cases of benign prostatic hypertrophy.

ultrasound: use of high-frequency sound waves to image various body organs.

urethra: the tube that carries urine from the bladder to the penis.

urine flow rate: the speed and amount of urine expelled; used to help determine if urethra is obstructed.

urologist: medical doctor specially trained to investigate and treat disorders of the prostate, bladder, kidney, and other urinary-tract organs.

vacuum-assisted erection device: device that helps men achieve and maintain an erection.

Velban: see *vinblastine sulfate*.

Velsar: see *vinblastine sulfate*.

vinblastine sulfate (Velban, Velsar): chemotherapy treatment used for advanced prostate cancer.

watchful waiting: a "wait-and-see" approach, in which a doctor continues to monitor symptoms of benign prostatic hypertrophy or prostate cancer without recommending a specific treatment until it is necessary.

zinc: a trace element essential for normal growth and for normal functioning of the prostate gland. Zinc is found in lean meat, whole-grain breads, and cereals.

Zoladex: see *goserelin*.

Appendix

SOURCES OF HELP

American Cancer Society
National Headquarters
1599 Clifton Road N.E.
Atlanta, GA 30329
(800) ACS-2345
  The Society is a voluntary, community-based organization offering service programs such as transportation to doctor's visits, rehabilitation programs such as the "Look Good . . . Feel Better" program, and a variety of educational materials. Call the 800 number or your local division.

American Foundation for Urologic Disease
1120 N. Charles St. #401
Baltimore, MD 21201
(800) 242-AFUD
  Provides brochures on benign prostatic hypertrophy and male urinary problems, prostatitis, prostate cancer.

Cancer Information Service

(800) 4-CANCER

Cancer information specialists can answer questions and send free brochures.

Among the titles:

"What You Need to Know about Prostate Cancer"

"Research Report: Cancer of the Prostate"

"Services Available for People with Cancer—National and Regional Organizations"

"When Cancer Recurs: Meeting the Challenge Again"

"Eating Hints: Recipes and Tips for Better Nutrition during Cancer Treatment"

"Answers to Your Questions about Metastatic Cancer"

"Radiation Therapy and You: A Guide to Self-Help during Treatment"

National Cancer Institute

Office of Cancer Communications

Bethesda, MD 20892

The federal National Cancer Institute offers the brochure "Cancer of the Prostate Research Report" and other educational materials on chemotherapy, management of localized prostate cancer, and clinical trials.

Community Hospital Programs

Contact your community hospital and ask if it sponsors any support groups or informational meetings. Some, for instance, cosponsor an "I Can Cope with Cancer" series, consisting of ten weekly classes for people with cancer. The sessions touch on daily health concerns, information about the disease, understanding emotions, nutritional aspects, enhancement of self-esteem and sexuality, support systems.

Other hospitals offer guest speakers, such as physicians and other health-care providers who specialize in cancer treatment.

National Council Against Health Fraud
PO Box 1276
Loma Linda, CA 92354
A nonprofit voluntary health agency that focuses on health fraud, misinformation, and quackery as public health problems. It will provide information on questionable cancer methods.

National Second Surgical Opinion Program Hotline
(800) 638-6833
Sponsored by the Health Care Financing Administration, U.S. Department of Health and Human Services. Helps locate specialists to provide a second opinion.

Simon Foundation
(800) 23-SIMON
The hotline provides a free patient education packet on urinary incontinence, which can be a side effect of prostate cancer treatment.

Vital Options
4419 Coldwater Canyon Avenue
Suite A
Studio City, CA 91604
(818) 508-5657
Support groups, based in Los Angeles and San Fran-

cisco, for young adults (up to mid forties) with cancer, their families, and friends.

Wellness Community
2200 Colorado Ave.
Santa Monica, CA 90404-3504
(310) 453-2200

Network of programs designed for people with cancer and their families. Founded in 1982. Ten locations in northern and southern California; Knoxville, Tennessee; Chicago, Illinois; Cincinnati, Ohio. Locations planned in Boston, Massachusetts; Anne Arundel County and Baltimore, Maryland; Philadelphia, Pennsylvania; St. Louis, Missouri. Promotes patient involvement in healing. A nonprofit organization, the Wellness Community offers informal drop-in discussion groups; participant groups facilitated by therapists; family groups; training in relaxation and visualization; workshops; nutrition information; exercise programs; social events and other activities.

ADDITIONAL READING

Benson, Herbert, and Miriam Z. Klipper. *The Relaxation Response.* New York: Avon Books, 1976.

Borysenko, Joan. *Minding the Body, Mending the Mind.* Redding, Mass.: Addison-Wesley Publishing Company, Inc., 1987.

Cousins, Norman. *Anatomy of an Illness.* New York: W. W. Norton & Company, 1979.

Fiore, Neil, Ph.D. *The Road Back to Health: Coping with the Emotional Aspects of Cancer.* New York: Bantam Books, 1984.

Siegel, Bernie S. *Love, Medicine, and Miracles.* New York: Harper & Row, 1986.

ABOUT CLINICAL TRIALS

To find out more about clinical trial for prostate cancer, call the National Cancer Institute's Cancer Information Service, (800) 4-CANCER. The call is toll free; a trained counselor will answer questions.

WHAT IS PDQ?

PDQ, or Physicians Data Query, is a computer system that provides up-to-date information on cancer treatment. The system is a service of the National Cancer Institute for people with cancer and their family members and for physicians, nurses, and other health-care professionals. By accessing PDQ information, you can find out about current treatments for prostate cancer and most other cancers. The information is reviewed monthly by cancer experts and updated when warranted.

To obtain the information by fax, simply call the PDQ System, (301) 402-5874, and when instructed enter the code for patient information for prostate cancer: #201229. You will receive a half dozen or more pages outlining information about prostate cancer, and a treatment option overview for each stage.

NEW DRUGS: THE ROUTE TO MARKET

It can take a dozen years or longer for a drug to work its way through the pipeline from research to market, according to the Pharmaceutical Manufacturers Association. Here is what is involved.

Preclinical testing can take about three and a half years. In this stage, scientists work in the laboratory and with animals, trying to determine if the substance under study is safe and biologically active.

Human clinical testing can take six years or more, during which time researchers must prove the safety and effectiveness of the drug. Often, more than three thousand volunteer patients are studied. Next, a manufacturer files a new drug application with the Food and Drug Administration and waits for approval, which can take about two and a half years.

HOW TO TALK WITH YOUR DOCTOR

How effectively you talk to your doctor might depend on how effectively you organize your questions for the office visit. Dr. Richard Frankel, a sociolinguist at the University of Rochester School of Medicine and Dentistry on staff at Highland Hospital, says the first concern patients bring up is not necessarily the most important to them.

In his studies of patient-doctor interactions, he has found that patients have on average eighteen seconds to state their concerns before being interrupted by their physician.

To improve communication, he suggests patients take a list of questions to the doctor and to interrupt, courteously, when their physician does not address their concerns. Patients should also learn to present their concerns in order of importance—something few do now, research shows. All this communication takes very little extra time, says Frankel. In his studies, patients given an opportunity to ask all their questions lengthened the office visit by only about a minute.

Other tips from health-care professionals about improving doctor-patient communication:

- Write down your questions as they occur to you.

- Ask your doctor to include your questions in your chart.

- If your doctor talks too fast, ask him or her to slow down. If you don't understand the medical terms, say so.

- Ask if your doctor has any videotapes that you could borrow to find out more about your cancer and/or treatment.

SECOND OPINIONS

Before you consent to an operation or other procedure, you might wish to obtain a second opinion. In fact, your doctor may even suggest getting a second opinion and refer you to another specialist or a cancer center. Your insurance plan may require a second opinion before consenting to reimbursement.

Materials such as X rays, blood tests, and other data will be released to the physician providing the consultation and second opinion.

Do not worry that getting a second opinion will unduly delay your treatment. Prostate cancer is usually slow growing, and you should explore all options and be sure that your ultimate choice of therapy is best for you.

If your doctor does not refer you, and you want a second opinion, call the local county medical society, the nearest cancer center, or your local American Cancer Society office to find a doctor for a second opinion.

Another route is to look up a specialist in the *Directory of Medical Specialists,* a reference volume available at many public libraries.

Some patients are tempted to get a second opinion without telling the doctor who made the original diagnosis. That is usually unwise, since the doctor providing the second exam needs all information already gathered. It is not likely your doctor will be offended by your seeking a second opinion.

Ask your doctor and the doctor giving you a second opinion:

- What are the benefits of the treatment recommended?

- What complications should be expected, if any? What are the risks?

- What would happen if this treatment was not given?

- Is there another option?

- What hospitalization time will probably be needed?

- What effect will the treatment have on potency?

- What effect will it have on urinary function?

PREPARING FOR AN OPERATION: ANESTHESIA, INFORMED CONSENT

If you and your doctor decide an operation is needed, knowing what to expect can reduce anxiety. Below are general points about anesthesia, suggestions on how best to prepare for an operation, and details about the "informed consent" form you will be asked to sign.

If you undergo surgery, you will be given anesthesia—either general (whole-body), local, regional ("spinal"), or some combination of these methods. Before the operation, the anesthesiologist will meet with you to describe the procedure to be followed. Either an anesthesiologist or a nurse-anesthetist working under a doctor's supervision will administer the anesthesia and remain with you for the entire operation.

An anesthesiologist is a medical doctor who has completed four years of residency in anesthesiology and related specialties. Most hospitals and physician groups require an anesthesiologist to be board certified.

A nurse-anesthetist, also called a certified registered nurse-anesthetist, has completed four years of nursing school, another year of critical-care nursing, and two years of postgraduate study in anesthesia. A nurse-anesthetist must be board certified and take recertification courses biannually. She or he always works under the supervision of a physician.

Preparing for an operation can make things go more smoothly. Whichever procedure you and your doctor choose, try to arrive at the hospital feeling as rested as possible. Before an operation it is a good idea to avoid aspirin (Bufferin, Anacin, Alka-Seltzer, and so on) for at least two weeks, since it can inhibit the blood's clotting function and increase the risk of bleeding.

If you undergo an operation or certain other procedures, you will be asked to sign an "informed consent" form. The consent form often includes a thorough explanation of the procedure and the risks involved. Your signature confirms that you understand the operation, that all your questions have been answered, and that you agree to undergo it. You need to weigh the risks of the operation against the hoped-for benefits.

Index

About the Authors

Charles E. Shapiro, M.D., is a board-certified urologist and a fellow of the prestigious American College of Surgeons. For the past decade, he has practiced urology in Los Angeles. He is also a clinical assistant professor of urology at the University of Southern California.

Dr. Shapiro speaks frequently to community groups on the topic of men's health and cancer prevention. He has published numerous scientific articles in the *Journal of Urology* and other medical journals and speaks frequently to colleagues at medical meetings on a variety of urologic topics.

He is a member of the American Urological Association, the American Fertility Society, the International Microsurgical Society, the California Medical Association, the Los Angeles County Medical Association, and the Los Angeles Urological Society, among others. He graduated Phi Beta Kappa from the University of California, Berkeley, and received his medical degree from Stanford University. He also trained in urology at Stanford University.

He resides in Los Angeles with his wife, Lesley, and son, Alexander.

Kathleen Doheny is an independent journalist specializing in health and behavior topics. She writes a weekly personal health column and a twice-monthly travel health column for the *Los Angeles Times.* She also contributes to the *Times*'s health supplement, "View" section, and Sunday magazine. She is contributing editor for *Men's Fitness* magazine and has written for *The Washington Post,* the *Chicago Tribune, Allure* magazine, *Omni* magazine, *Fitness* magazine, *First* magazine, and *Modern Maturity,* among others. Her articles are frequently syndicated by the Los Angeles Times Syndicate or the Los Angeles Times's Health and Fitness News Service. She has experience as a radio health-show cohost, a general-assignment newspaper reporter, and a medical editor.

Doheny received a bachelor's degree in journalism from Ball State University and a certificate in broadcast journalism from UCLA. She resides in Burbank, California, with her son, Shaun Newton.